# *In Like Company*
## The *Salt River Review* & *Porch* Anthology

Edited by James Cervantes

MadHat Press
Asheville, North Carolina

MadHat Press
MadHat Incorporated
PO Box 8364, Asheville, NC 28814

All contents are copyright © 2015 their respective authors and artists. All rights reserved.

The Library of Congress has assigned this edition a Control Number of 2015902989

ISBN 978-1-941196-14-4 (paperback)

Book and cover design by MadHat Press

Divider image: *Hammakka* by Arturo Desimone

www.MadHat-Press.com

First Printing

# IN LIKE COMPANY

The *Salt River Review*
& *Porch* Anthology

*In Like Company*

# CONTENTS

| | |
|---|---|
| *Afternoon Preface* <br> Pamela Stewart | xv |
| *Introduction* <br> James Cervantes | xvii |

## POETRY

| | |
|---|---|
| **Liz Ahl** <br> Trajectories | 3 |
| **Pamela Alexander** <br> Who Stayed | 5 |
| **Carlos Drummond de Andrade** <br> Interpretation of December, <br>    *translated by Mark Strand* | 7 |
| **Wendy Battin** <br> Elementals | 11 |
| **Gaston Baquero** <br> The River, <br>    *translated by Greg Simon & Steven F. White* | 14 |
| **Johannes Beilharz** <br> There is a chance I may not have been Jeremiah | 15 |
| **Mario Benedetti** <br> Haiku, <br>    *translated by Carlos Reyes* | 17 |
| **James Bertolino** <br> Tuxedo Psychosis | 20 |
| **Ankur Betageri** <br> Ignorance | 21 |
| **Peter Bruveris** <br> The Last Galindian Soldier, <br>    *translated by Inara Cedrins* | 22 |

The *Salt River Review* & *Porch* Anthology

**Michael Burkard**
Conversation With Robert Wald                         25
Odd Hours                                             27

**Rebecca Byrkit**
The Available Country of Women                        29

**Wendy Taylor Carlisle**
Parsing the *Noli Me Tangere*                         30

**Alex Cigale**
Man, who seeks to be nothing but himself              31

**Peter Cooley**
Descant                                               33

**Flavia Cosma**
Winter Again                                          34

**Pablo Antonio Cuadra**
The Mango Tree,                                       35
    *translated by Greg Simon & Steven F. White*

**Catherine Daly**
Howrah Bridge: Rabindra Setu                          40

**Rubén Darío**
fragment from Santa Elena De Montenegro,              41
    *translated by Greg Simon & Steven F. White*

**Gonçalves Dias**
Song of Exile,                                        43
    *translated by Greg Simon*

**Norman Dubie**
M's Last Notes for the Lacrimosa                      45
There Is a Dream Dreaming Us                          47

**Joseph Duemer**
Clutter                                               50

**Simon Peter Eggertsen**
Twelve Questions in One Long Sentence                 52

**Paul Éluard**
An Apologia for Knowledge VI  53
Closer to Us,  53
*translated by Peter Robertson*

**Skip Fox**
Whatever Thing Death Be  54
Blood in Black and White  55

**Suzanne Frischkorn**
Chrysalis  56

**Tess Gallagher**
The Women of Auschwitz  58
Let's Store These Hours  62

**John Gilgun**
Cold Morning  64

**Larry Goodell**
Goddess of the Big Bang  65

**David Graham**
Heaven Changes  66

**John Haines**
Watching the Fire II  68

**H. Palmer Hall**
The Car Hop at Sonic  70

**Ed Harkness**
Transitioning  72

**Charles O. Hartman**
Puddle System  74

**Jim Heavily**
Sonnets for Two Women  76

**Bob Herz**
Winner Takes All  78

**Dennis Hinrichsen**
Living in the Other World  80

**Cynthia Hogue**
"the good," from *In June, the Labyrinth* — 82

**Christopher Howell**
Flood — 84

**Gray Jacobik**
The Power Outage — 86

**Laura Jensen**
My Father At Times — 87
A Poem and What a Poem Has Become — 88

**Halvard Johnson**
Schattenwelt — 89

**Jesse Lee Kercheval**
Japanese Expedition to Antarctica, 1911–1912 — 90

**Federico García Lorca**
Widow of the Moon, — 91
  *translated by Greg Simon*

**John Morgan**
A Renaissance Altarpiece — 93

**Peter Munro**
Elegy For What Falls — 95

**Sheila Murphy**
Lauds (11) — 96

**Pablo Neruda**
Torrid Ode, — 97
  *translated by Greg Simon*

**Sergio Ortiz**
Only the Rumor — 99

**Sam Pereira**
The Blue Scent of Juniper — 101
Method — 103

**Ignacio Ruiz Perez**
Self-Portrait Of Coleridge 104
Billy Budd Enchained, 105
   *translated by Carlos Reyes*

**Doug Ramspeck**
Tupelos 106

**Rochelle Ratner**
Steps 108

**Carlos Reyes**
Snake 109

**Tad Richards**
Evolution 111

**Mary Ruefle**
Suddenly 113
All This, All This 114

**Jim Simmerman**
Tell The Truth 115

**Greg Simon**
Song [Self-Analysis] 117
Song [The Slivers] 118

**David Starkey**
The Incredulous Midwife 120
The Healing of the Blind Man 121

**Pamela Stewart**
*If Translation* 122
The Same Window 123

**Carolyn Stoloff**
Lorca's Silence 124

**Lynn Strongin**
"The Magpie is a Most Illustrious Bird" 125

**Jeanie Thompson**
To Lesbos 128

**Marina Tsvetaeva**
Five Poems, 132
    *translated by Alex Cigale*

**Liliana Ursu**
The Sand of Olimp 135
A Path to the Sea, or the Letter *A*, 136
    *translated by the poet, Adam J. Sorkin & Tess Gallagher*

**Roger Weingarten**
Self-Portrait as The Magnificent Frigatebird 137

**Steven F. White**
Under Her Window: Ouro Prêto 140

## Fiction

**Roberta Allen**
Every Man's Nightmare 145

**Jay Baruch**
A Little Heart 146

**Charles Blackstone**
37% 156

**Lee Byrd**
Lazy Heart of Mine 162

**Rochelle Cashdan**
Rescuers 184

**Tania Casselle**
The Trials of Summer 189

**Avital Gad Cykman**
Soap 191

**Jesse Dorris**
The Alabama Station 193

**Hugh Fox**
Genealogy 203

**Anne Germanacos**
Saying I love you in a variety of ways                209

**Terri Lee Hackman**
Bunny Ears                                            220

**Tsipi Keller**
Spiders                                               222

**Edith Konecky**
Margo on the Beach                                    224

**Nathan Leslie**
It Can't Hurt, Can It?                                228

**Norman Lock**
from *Pieces for a Small Orchestra*                   236

**Carol Novack**
Dance, Baby, Dance                                    240

**Tim Poland**
Brazilian Mahogany                                    242

**Tiffany Promise**
Every Hollow Thing                                    246

**Carole Rosenthal**
Fusion                                                249

**Max Ruback**
Sand                                                  257

**Thaddeus Rutkowski**
City Visit                                            260

**Lynda Schor**
Failure of Vision                                     266

**Icy Sedgwick**
The Thwarted Stalker                                  271

**Gail Louise Siegel**
Habit                                                 274

The *Salt River Review* & *Porch* Anthology

**Emeniano Acain Somoza**
My Lost Siquijor   276

**Girija Tropp**
Godmother of Trash   288

**Donna D. Vitucci**
Rupture   290

**Zachary Watterson**
The Prophet   294

**Kulpreet Yadav**
All You Need is One Good Shot   296

## Coda

*What The Dormouse Said: Take Time To Read,*
*It Is the Fountain of Wisdom*   303
Laura Jensen

## Contributors' Biographies   309

*In Like Company*

# AFTERNOON PREFACE

It's one of the last stretch-out-beneath-the shade-tree days of summer.

I sit, feet bared to the wind, wondering how many poems I might have read and misread over the last (yikes!) 50 years. The noisy crows downfield are concentrating on scaring off a red-tailed hawk. They remind me that as the world goes about its business poems are being written and read everywhere on earth.

How fortunate one is to be able to read and hear poetry, to sing it, hold it close to the heart, offer it to another. This receiving/reading of poems is both flexible and unpredictable. So is poetry itself and the spirits of both are in alliance; I couldn't live without them.

For reasons almost beyond me, I lived in Arizona in the '70s and when *Porch* (magazine) also arrived, accompanied by editor Jim Cervantes, it became the first literary magazine I ever *watched*. How it prevailed, assembled like a great meal, was something I came to respect deeply. I really cared about it! Later, the *Salt River Review* was the first on-line publication I ever encountered and I squiggled up my nose wondering if being on-line meant it was actually *real*. By golly, it sure was.

How strong today's late August breeze and the first tinting out of green along the hills. Now, before my eyes is an invitation of voices, this beautiful anthology flaring its stories and poems which also includes a fine selection of poetry in translation.

Another pleasure is that a fair number of poems included here are *new work*.

Tone, flavor, cadence, *heart*—in a poem they all recognize each other. And here, while the arrangement is sensibly alphabetical, the pieces are so well selected that the effect is that of orchestration. The prose which follows enhances the book's structure with the embrace of a retaining wall. The fiction here is various—from traditional structures to the oddball, intuitive declarations of Anne Germanacos' "Saying I Love You in a Variety of Ways." The arraying of writing is exhilarating!

As a reader, eating words with my eyes, I am part that "child suspended in memory" introduced in Carlos Drummond de Andrade's 'Interpretation of December' (translated by Mark Strand.) She's a busy child!

As we read, voices rise across time and circumstance, from the days when we all smoked cigarettes to when we mostly don't, from Iron City beer and bologna sandwiches, to oatmeal and 1% milk for breakfast. The poems and stories fly through wars, losses, space travel, broken marriages, births—whatever it's all made of—for us and the crows. This gathering up makes the book feel *local*. Readers and writers at home together.

As the afternoon pulls tighter along the horizon, the crows keep at their business and I wonder if the intensity and timelessness of poetry itself could please these clever birds. Perhaps they are always reciting for us. Poems and stories may be clever, instinctual, 'well-wrought,' or mostly musical—but it's always more than artifice; even the most despairing writing is made from, and of, life itself. "It is the child in us/ or outside us/harvesting the myth." Those lines from 'Interpretation of December' are, in part, my path into this anthology; those children might be the writers, readers, the editors. It's all three which both make and celebrate *In Like Company*.

*—Pamela Stewart, August 2014, Hawley, MA*

# INTRODUCTION

In his Afterword to the final issue of *The Salt River Review*, Greg Simon wrote: "If our deadlines were the conventional ones of time and space, the principle was ethereal ... somewhere beyond but not excluding words, where poems line up and become greater than themselves in like company." He was speaking of *Porch*, the print magazine and precursor to *The Salt River Review*, although the principle held through the early and problematic days of electronic publication and guided the selections for this anthology.

Without *Porch* (1977–1981), *The Salt River Review* (1997–2010) would not have existed. We would not have learned how to be editors in the larger sense. There would not have been a core of poets to spread the word and follow us from one medium to another. The difference between the two magazines is that fiction writers have joined the poets who have been with us for thirty-three years of publishing. Another difference is that the sheer number of poets and poems we have published dictated that now their appearance would be ordered and presented according to the poet's last name, depriving *me* somewhat of the intrinsic joy of orchestrating their voices—or at least the comforting illusion that I could be doing that.

Since this odyssey began with a print magazine founded in Seattle, it was fitting that the inception of *In Like Company* occurred at the 2014 AWP conference in Seattle when Alex Cigale asked me if I'd be interested in doing a printed anthology of work by poets and writers from *The Salt River Review*—it seems he and others had just been talking about SRR. What a pleasant surprise to learn that the online magazine was still mentioned and respected!

I had a similar surprise shortly before deciding to end the review's thirteen-year run when I heard from someone who "wanted to know what all the buzz was about," and who had been disappointed that *SRR* was not technically flashy and seemed to be "just an electronic version of a print magazine." I wrote back that the quality of writing was what the buzz was probably about. I had to confess, also, that our technical staff and resources were limited, i.e. myself, my enduring friends, a keyboard, a free and outdated html program, and my pending retirement. But it was nice to learn there was a "buzz."

*In Like Company* includes new work from those who chose us as we chose them in the early days of their careers: Norman Dubie, Michael Burkard, Mary Ruefle, Tess Gallagher, Pamela Stewart, John Morgan, Cynthia Hogue, Joseph Duemer, Christopher Howell, Ed Harkness, Laura Jensen, and many others. Thanks to Greg Simon, *SRR* continued to feature poetry in translation and this volume includes selections from *Porch* and *SRR*, as well as new translations from Carlos Reyes and Inara Cedrins. This volume also remembers those whom we published in both magazines and who have left us in the intervening years: Hugh Fox (1932–2011), John Haines (1924–2011), H. Palmer Hall (1942–2013), Carol Novack (1948–2011), Rochelle Ratner (1949–2008), and Jim Simmerman (1952–2006).

My sincere thanks here to Greg Simon and Lynda Schor for editorial assistance, and to Alex Cigale, Jonathan Penton, and Marc Vincenz of MadHat Press, for providing the occasion for this anthology. What this means to me and the poets and writers was perhaps best expressed by Laura Jensen when I requested permission to use her essay, "What The Dormouse Said," as the Coda to this volume: *How terribly interesting that you want to include my essay in the anthology.... I am very flattered, exactly as we would feel long ago when work was wanted. Thanks so much. I wonder where those associations with publishing came from, the reification of the time suspended nowhere but with the piece.* And so here we are, suspended *In Like Company*.

—James Cervantes, September 2014, San Miguel de Allende

# Poetry

# Liz Ahl

## TRAJECTORIES
### —Apollo 13

To make it home, they had to keep
hurtling away from Earth, gathered by gravity
into lunar orbit, the dark side never
quite this dark before.

Until the final burn they wouldn't be allowed
to hold Earth in the window, where it belonged,
to burst towards it rather than let it fade
over their shoulders, shrinking to moon-size.

They had to turn their backs on home
and trust the stripped-down physics
of momentum and return. They had to surrender
to the old forces and attractions.

To make it home, they had to fly away
from every instinct urging them to turn
around right there, as if the crippled craft
could turn on such a thin dime.

They had to believe in the machine,
that the spindly lunar lander as lifeboat
could do everything it wasn't designed to do—
like them, it was supposed to go to the moon.

The nature of the adventure shifted
from the journey to the return—coming home
was the new, untried frontier
as Cronkite called the play-by-play.

To make it home, they had to resurrect
the old imperatives, re-enter the race
that had already been run and won,
they had to want to make it home
like they wanted to make it to the moon.

# Pamela Alexander

## WHO STAYED

My little boy, cat in his arms,
sucked out the window

like he'd finally learned to fly.
Such noise, I couldn't hear

the silence when it came
or my bones creak when I stood.

Room too bright, wrong-
headed light. Mailbox

on my bed: my neighbor's. Hail
then rain, a downpour

inside, or what used to be.
Front door made of air.

Trees pale, bark blown off. Truck
snagged in a sycamore, radio

belting out *Busted flat in Baton Rouge*—
No walls, so no windows

or else windows everywhere.
Like an ordinary day my son

walked home. Shirt gone, cat gone,
words. Light stood around with us

like transparent trees, like houses
wanting to be rebuilt. Our friends,

everyone we knew, were they
ever here? Who are we now?

Who stayed, who was taken: not
judgment. Beyond personal.

The ones who stayed, we'll
catch up. We're right behind.

*In Like Company*

# Carlos Drummond de Andrade
*Translated from the Portuguese by Mark Strand*

## INTERPRETATION OF DECEMBER

Maybe it's the child
suspended in memory.
Two lit candles
in the depths of the room.
And the Jewish face
in the print, maybe.
The smell of various burners
under each pot.
Holy feet walking
in snow, in the backlands,
in the imagination.

The doll broken
before it was played with,
also a wheel
in the garden somewhere,
and the iron train
passing over me
so lightly: it doesn't crush me,
but remembers me instead.

It is the letter written
with difficult letters,
mailed at a post office
without stamp or approval.
The open window

where wandering eyes
lean out,
eyes that ask
and don't know how to give.

The old man sleeping
in the wrong chair.
The torn newspaper.
The dog pointing.
The cockroach scurrying.
The smell of cake.
The wind blowing.
And the clock stopped.
More litany of the mass
than can be suppressed,
the white dress
in a white street
flying back to the cold.
The hidden sweetness,
the forbidden book,
the frustrated bath,
the failed victory,
the dream of dancing
over a floor of water
or that voyage upon
the vastness of time
where the oldest laws
are never reached.

It is loneliness
in front of the chestnut trees,
the dull zone
in the sphere of sound,
the winestain
in the drunken towel,
displeasure of five hundred
mouths swallowing
false candy
still moist
from the weeping streets.

The empty hut
in the land without music.
The shared silence
in the land of ants.
The sleep of lizards
that never hear the bell.
Talk of fish
about things liquid.
Stories of the spider
at war with mosquitoes.
Stains of cut
and rotten wood.
Stinginess of stone
in a dull monologue.
The mine of mica
and the figurehead.

The natural night
without enchantment.
Something irreducible
in the life-giving legends
yet incorporated
in the heart of myth.

It is the child in us
or outside us
harvesting myth.

# Wendy Battin

## Elementals

Only the top of the periodic chart
of possible marriages matters here.
Silicon beach, the iron in it
drawing lines in the sand, and ocean
$H_2O$ with every spice in its soup.
A suit of water walking here
on her calcium rack rests
now in a tide pool under the hydrogen
sun, thinks
better of it with magnesium
brain which burns a blinding white
when a flame finds it.

\*

The day of the dead falls in summer
this year, Everyone's here, parents and sister

and friends, in this empty room, consuming the air.
My too-many selves. The elderly cat. The books

and the marriage gone wrong. I have nothing
to say, and I say it. How like a tale

it might be told. Red hood or white cloak,
a passage from Janacek, a bearded

stranger one morning behind you suddenly
clutching, foreign lands, then suddenly

age, the sage of being alone, the
nowhere to go now.

\*

When it's not the the moon but the headlights of an SUV
in the dark, the squeal that says I'm turning into your street
and it does, the asphalt is gone, there's metal flashing and nowhere
to cross, Don't Walk, Don't Walk, that orange hand held high,
I stay on the stoop, yes here there are stoops, and you
are miles away. It stays. The minutes years. I age,
go gray. When the red taillights with third eye bright
as the devil pass, it's too late, I've seen the cloven
prints and breathed the sulphur in.

\*

You can wipe the memory
from your phone, as if you'd never spoken.
Wipe your hard drive. Burn your poems.
Some government remembers
but you aren't a person of interest
or not so much. The word is still
in the river, caught
in the tide pools but cut
loose when the water rises..

\*

*In Like Company*

The last question and then
the test is over. What will you do
when you're dead? Knit,
if you don't. There's no end to knitting.
Go on speaking into the silence
as if it were keepsake.
Take care of the cat,
the cat is still alive, and so
too a man, no rest
when the world ends.

# Gastón Baquero

*Translated from the Spanish by Greg Simon & Steven F. White*

## The River

*for Josè Olivio Jimènez*

I've spent sixty years on the banks of a river.
Only those who are living there can see it.
People heading toward the western market
looked at us with fear. They don't understand
why the dampness would cling to our clothing,
or how we'd reel in those fish for them,
the color of blood oranges,
from the invisible water.

One day a man fell in, and did not reappear.
Passers-by, interrupting errands to the market,
exclaimed, "Where did he go?"
"When is he coming back?"
and, "How marvelous, those fiery yellow fish!"
Those of us born to the river kept quiet.
Smiled enigmatically. Said nothing. Gave no sign.
The language of our tribe is silence.
We wanted to protect our invisible river.
On its banks
the world belonged to us—
as did its mystery.

# Johannes Beilharz

## THERE IS A CHANCE I MAY NOT HAVE BEEN JEREMIAH

So I tolerate ridicule for years,
having grown my beard long and wild
and wearing ancient Aramaic garb
(which is hard to come by, by the way,
and not pleasant to wear due to coarseness
and itching) and calling out the truth of the Lord
with my increasingly hoarse voice,

and my old friend suffers the same for knowing
and openly admitting that he is
the second coming of John the Baptist,
so we decide to prove the truth for once and all,
to ourselves at least if not to the masses
of unbelievers abounding nowadays, by doing a regression.

We listen around and finally hear about someone
to trust and phone to make an appointment,
go there at the appointed hour, sit in the waiting room
a bit, finally get our turn one-by-one. He tells me
to follow the pendulum with my eyes, to only do that,
not think of anything else, and I do it and eventually
arrive at that weird state in which I know I still have
a body but can also look down at myself from outside,

and later it all deepens, a hole opens, I slip through
after some hesitation and know I'm in different times,
but all I see is grassland and sheep and a glimpse
of a dog, get rained on, feel dryness and heat, eat
sheep meat and lentils someone brings me, only that,
nothing of Babylon and its armies, of whom I'd
supposedly prophesied to my people, no-one like
Nebuchadnezzar, whom I would have liked to see,

no, just sheep and grass and dry land and ravines
and desert and a puddle of water here and there.
And the strange thing is that my friend tells me
later he saw exactly the same. No baptizing
of people in the Jordan and staying in the desert
for 30 days on a diet of locusts. No: sheep,
herding them, cleaning them, slaughtering them,
suffering heat and dryness with them, walking
with them. Well, maybe we were shepherds
together. Maybe. Maybe repeatedly.

# Mario Benedetti
*Translated from the Spanish by Carlos Reyes*

## Haiku

if the heart
gets bored with loving
what's it good for?

\*

hey hey!
passing girl
kiss my soul

\*

in every idyll
there is a mouth that kisses
and one that is kissed

\*

every woman
can be two women
I'll settle for just one

\*

the girls stroll along
with each step they get more beautiful
and me older

\*

those legs of hers
left us speechless
feeling old, wrinkled

\*

in love
it is virtuous to be faithful
but not fanatic

\*

I don't want to see you
for the rest of the year
or at least not until Tuesday

\*

in the middle of the night
if my hands call you
your breasts come

\*

the peace of whorehouses
does not harm
true love

\*

when seducing us
women turn into
guitars

\*

*In Like Company*

I'm not seduced
by the bordello of power
I prefer the other one

\*

it's the crazy hands
of the pianist and blacksmith
that speak to us

\*

bombings
remedy forever
thirst and hunger

\*

in 2000
we will have six missiles
for every crow

\*

it was the arms
of Venus de Milo
that were applauding

# James Bertolino

## Tuxedo Psychosis

The small, brutal captives
have evolved as
our major
concern.

We thought their formal dress
a convenient
oppression

But now what approaches
like an oily fog
to threaten
this clinical delicacy

will be described only as
"Freudness peculiar"—

the classic case of mongrel duty.

We must at all costs
crush this
surly convention.

They will be rescued
by atrocities
of denim

& the disciplines of lust.

# Ankur Betageri

## IGNORANCE

What does the day know about
the golden ray which has illumined it?

What do the eyes know about the light
which has encircled them?

Does the mango-blossom know what it has done
to the koel*?

Does the mind which wakes from one blue morning into another
know which turbulent cloud it slept in when it dreamt?

Summer which rains on everyone's face
does it know in whose face it has become a lightning?

If this girl
is the cause of my ecstasy and distress—

who built her like a nest of all the skies
that the bird in my heart
wants to fly in?

---
\* koel: the Indian cuckoo

# Peter Bruveris
*Translated from the Latvian by Inara Cedrins*

## The Last Galindian Soldier

Fog, fog, thick and dim all around and crackling underbrush,
and branches striking face, under bare
feet the terrible sway of the swamp;
each bush like a dead man arching a bow,
each marshy pool like an eye wordlessly sucking into eternity;

ai fog, frozen for eternity in the pupil of the eye,
ai treacherous fog mother,
ai thunder, about your ankles twists
yarn the color of curdled blood
in whose strands
are the souls of my slain brothers;

ai mother, your lullaby catches in my throat,
I've forgotten horses, who don't know the order of battle,
forgotten girls, who come toward one smiling hopefully;

ai mother, this endless bush, this enmity dimmed breath,

this half-numbed hand
and two lone feet, under which death squelches;
and my father hopelessly lost,
in a black jackdaw screaming above fog, above hollow fir trees,
ai this grizzled grass all about,
which like the hair of a moaning priest
throws loops around the feet—

*In Like Company*

MUTE WATER GETS INTO MY MOUTH
BLINDNESS STICKS TO MY EYES

what lows there, what shimmers,
what slips there through fog?
seems like—birch bark trumpets
and bagpipes under arms,
dimmed faces …

north wind blows ice over pools in the marsh
and bites into bones
(birches wail),
as the fog disperses over the swamp
like a bloodied colt's head the Sun rises;

along with the fog we slip away,
away to the fields of forgetfulness,
away as faint reflections
in mirrors of the future,
inexplicably echoing
in oak hollows,

our song
will revert to the rustling of birches
and incessant weeping rain,
our piping will die to whispers
in dry reeds,
fog will take us and not give us back,
we will no longer be with you—

and only in those damp nights
when rain causes the earth to grow heavy and impossible to
    wade through,
like a sword's stroke I will
ache in the small of your back

# Michael Burkard

## Conversation With Robert Wald

I was sitting with R., and I was reading Szymborska
and I told R. I had written a poem because of something
Mary Hackett had said—I think she was talking about life
in Washington D.C.—one reason she got tired of it—and
I told R. Mary said "there were always too many people,
or too many bridges, or too many people with bridges on them."
And R. liked that—and laughed—and said is that what she said?
And then R. said "too many people with bridges on them."
And I said I like that—it's better than what I wrote, or it's more
interesting—What did you write R. asked, what did Mary say—
Oh, I said, she actually said "there were always too many people
or too many bridges or too many bridges with people on them."
And then I said I wrote a poem using that, called "Bridges with
People on Them." But it's never been in a book I said. I always
liked it I said. Then it was funny to me that years later a translation
of Szymborska's *People on a Bridge* appears—I didn't actually say
it quite like that to R.—but I wanted to read the poem to R.—
    and I did—and
because I was reading this aloud for the first time and because
I was reading it to R. it really moved me—for a moment in the
    small
light (although it was very bright outside the kitchen)—for a
    moment
I thought the poem was going to end at the bottom of the page,
page 3: *czas potknql sie i upadl* (page 2) time stumbled and fell—
but it went on another fifteen lines, and I was very glad the
    poem did,

because it moved me so to be reading this to R., and R. said something like I am very glad it went on too. I am very glad for Mary,
and for R., and for Szymborska—and for this little life book I wasn't even going to buy one day, but one day I did. And here is R., seeing a happy photograph of Wislawa pass before R's eyes upside down —but R. notices the happiness right away, and I turn the book to R. and Wislawa Szymborska is smiling a full smile, with her right hand beside her neck, with a very thick ring on her fourth finger.

# Odd Hours

Today I said it was tomorrow,
it had to be tomorrow
and the recently dead moon
played along with me.

Tomorrow became yesterday,
then last week and
the week before that—

My clocks were protesting—
each wanted as much involvement with this work
as the moon had agreed to,
despite consequences

My clocks reminded me of the time
I was visiting my brother,
who always managed to work odd hours—
and how one late afternoon
I opened the door to his bedroom
to see if he slept or not.
He slept. But his clocks—

Each was ticking off seconds
from corners in the room, and in shadowlight
I made out the main clock at his bedside—

But each clock was not in sync with
each other—it was like an orchestra
where everyone in the clock section
was assigned a different time to keep—

I grew dizzy at the unsyncopation—
Feeling that if I did not quietly leave
I might myself hear something
like my own heartbeat—
out of sync with every place of time—

My brother slept.

# Rebecca Byrkit

## THE AVAILABLE COUNTRY OF WOMEN
### *for Deni*

By the end of any appalling and brilliant day
In any Athenian winter, knocked out on an airplane bisecting
    the sea,

Exactly around the fire, a beautiful man or outrageous child
Or father from a longer place, says I would die for you.

Romancing a flame, crouching, crunching the ash, you either
Answer: I know, or you will, or you did. You

Wake, wild and typical as wheels touch down on fast black
    gravel. You want
Waffles early Sunday mornings from a mix. You want Miyake,
    birch-smooth skis,

A sun, a splintering sea. Irish Mist. You ask your dream, and
    mean it: Why not
*Live out on the earth like this?*

# Wendy Taylor Carlisle

## PARSING THE *NOLI ME TANGERE*

Jesus advises the Magdelene, *don't touch me*, as he quits
the tomb.  Her red skirt undulates below his feet.
He's carrying a hoe. He wears a Piedmont farmer's hat.

That's how a nameless artist pictures his Messiah,
as a peasant in a winding sheet, rocks tossed aside and in
the vacant chamber, the Madonna with an angel settled

nearby for company.  He renders Christ's wounded instep,
the tipped vial and adds Saint Francis in his brown robe, set there
to adore his Master with halo and rosary, his corner

of the composition blessed. After centuries of smoke
and blur the canvas' blues dull, some paint cracks, mostly
the background seems too dark. From this perspective,

the palm lifts as if to stop the woman's human hand.
Jesus seems cold, putting her off.  Yet I imagine His words
as His body rises: *Don't worry; I'll be waiting.*

# Alex Cigale

## Man, who seeks to be nothing but himself

> "... the desert is a country of madness."
> —Thomas Merton

Spare tires extra food and water a small
gas stove a sewing kit satellite phone ...
we made then checked and rechecked the list

Stuck in the desert having used up
the last of our water on the radiator
watching stacks of dollar bills blow away

With the sand and wind these are the lessons
we learned the single most important thing
to carry in the desert is the right attitude

Everything matters and nothing matters
events don't change people they only bring
out what is already in them bad decisions

Can lead to death the journey is important
not the destination the golden rule is
first to accept the desert way: "Let it be"

Radiators burst hours from the nearest road
someone gets a scorpion snake or spider bite
twists an ankle is overcome by heat or fatigue

People want to get from point A to point B
but sometimes fate gives them another path
the desert is a country of madness

Roads are wounds inflicted on the earth
that nature is always trying to heal
and man man seeks to be nothing but himself

# Peter Cooley

## Descant

First bird of morning—one singular blue note
against the sky, and now another one.

Why do you want to break into me like this,
a man who finds morning another night,

another kind of darkness, my blindness
the one that comes from too much radiance?

Little wings, keep your chorus to yourself.
I've learned to walk between the stars. And you?

# Flavia Cosma

## Winter Again

My eyes are filled with snow;
The moon's eyes are covered in mud;
Forgotten in the cupboard, a spoon of dross,
On the table's corner, enticing,
A glass full of hate.

Big cubes of ice tumble down into the void,
Crippled branches keep watch over deserted streets,
The snow creaks under unseen steps,
A white blanket mysteriously wraps
Putrefied, crimson leaves.

The season springs up and then dies;
Curses still linger in the rooms;
Time doesn't let itself be bought,
Either with silver coins, or with priceless treasures.

Oh, if only they would release us from our dream too,
Before spring arrived,
So that the ancient, celestial longings,
The rains' manes grown wild,
Streaming, wouldn't overcome us.

*In Like Company*

# Pablo Antonio Cuadra
*Translated from the Spanish by Greg Simon & Steven F. White*

## THE MANGO TREE

The lips that kissed you also told you,
"It's time for you to put down roots like the trees."
But you know about trees. You know about their different
        kinds of wood and growth rings.
Over the centuries, you've followed their slow caravans.
You've seen them in the jungles, by the great rivers,
their green hands covered with tangled vines and parasites,
fleeing into exile together with their birds. Fixed in space,
they make their pilgrimage. They are one invisible step
ahead of civilization.
You know about trees. You know
the native trees that helped to lift the land.
        River shepherds.
Trees that are so deeply Nicaraguan, like the pochotes,
which, even when slashed for kindling, sprout up again
        from the land.
And you know the strangers to this place
such as Senegal's abundant icaco tree,
or Algeria's pomegranate, or the immense breadfruit
        tree from the Moluccas,
or the mango that arrived in Nicaragua from distant Hindustan.

It was in Calcutta (or Kolkata) where the galleon reached port.
"A little more favorable wind and all of you will become rich
        and blessed with good fortune,"

says Captain Céspedes de Aldana. Then they altered their course
and crossed seven hundred churning leagues of the Gulf
of China or the Philippines in their galleon on the so-called
    "South Wind Journey."
There, the Captain found ivory and gold brocatelles, taffetas and
    damasks.
And as he brought a plant on board with its newly formed leaves,
the beautiful Hindu woman told him, "Let this tree
    bear witness to your pledges."
But people laughed and spoke about the affair in low voices,
everywhere, once Aunt Elisa and Aunt Mercedes had retired
    to their solemn chambers.
Aldana had rescued them from the gloom of spinsterhood
by bringing them to America, seasick, almost ruing
    their new bad fortune,
but bound for marriages of honor and profit.


At that time, Granada had two hundred inhabitants, mud-walled
    or lime-covered adobe buildings with ceramic roof tiles,
as well as a pretty church:
a fistful of salt in the vast tropical greenness.
And in Aldana's house, there was an astrolabe, a compass,
    and rolls of maps stained by seawater,
and the first clock brought from Germany, which he installed
like a tabernacle in a formal room
so the time it kept could guide the schedule for mass and
    meetings of the town council.
And in the courtyard, the mango tree, the first mango tree.

"I have heard," he would say, "that the learned Muslims claim
this fruit to be the avatar of a mysterious bird
called Jatayu,
bird-king of Hindustan,
red and black because the sun scorched its wings,
which means that it must be from the genus of the phoenix,
    from the Arabs, because it nests in fire."
    And the Indians
transmitted this legend, but changed it,
saying that Mango trees bear fruit to give back
the soul or yulio of the chichiltote bird,
the flaming votive bird of the Chorotegas.
And there was once a poet who sang of that fable:
"You can hear the song and laughter of the fruit
    beneath its skin."
On his first sweltering nights in Granada,
Aldana, that old wolf Juan Céspedes de Aldana,
always dressed in leather and suede, despite the heat,
    and wore
the featherless hood of the earliest sailors.
And he would weep as he thought of his faithful
47-ton caraval, "The Greyhound,"
built and armed by him with the proceeds
"from the many taxes he levied on the land he owned,"
and of its masts from Moguer, and his father, Don Alonso,
patriarch of the Pinzón family,
and of Diego de Lepe and Juan Díaz de Solís,
captains and pilots,
who were among the first to cross the equator
and who saw not only new lands but new stars as well.

And every time he harvested his mangoes,
as he passed around the fruit on a silver platter
    to his neighbors,
he would repeat the stories of his travails on his journeys:
On the perverse Sargasso Sea filled with ship-swallowing monsters
or on the passage through Guachinchina,
a gulf with many small hills and sandbanks,
replete with an Emperor and pearl divers,
or in the Philippines, where the women, Aldana said,
were incredibly chaste, with no conception of lust
or unfaithfulness to their husbands.
Then he would look at those who had gathered to hear him
and lower his booming pilot's voice
(he had the round ironic face of the Aldanas,
and their instincts, too, while his smile was a half-smile, really—
the rest of his sense of humor was in his eyes):
"She planted the seed during the full moon
and married the tree in her pagan rites, joining two branches.
Ah! She had the biggest and brightest eyes a man
    could ever see!"

But Felipillo, his knock-kneed dwarf servant,
added the detail that Yadira's breasts were anointed
    with sandalwood,
which made the heat bearable for the navigator.

His somewhat disillusioned grandchildren
inherited confusing chronicles, but could still read
the name of the plant in Sanskrit
in his diary with its yellowing pages,
and see drawings in ink from the Orient
of its polygamous flowers,

and its lanceolate leaves, dark green and shiny,
and the red fruit shaped like a heart. ("It will multiply
my heart," predicted the woman. And so it did,
    in thick bunches,
every time they made love.
With every heartbeat of the lovers,
more fruit came into being.) Now
not even one stone remains to mark the old patriarch.
He chose an impetuous land of history, heated to the point
    of calcination,
and filibuster William Walker's fires erased his name
when he burned the temple where Aldana
twice entered with bare feet to fulfill his pledges:
Once with a wax candle in his hand
when he lost his ship (after almost reaching home)
in a wind-whipped downpour on the Gulf of Papagayo,
and then again as a corpse,
wearing a Franciscan robe and hood.

The mango tree also burned its story in time:
and now you consider it from this place.
It professes a familiar green,
was born in your islands,
accompanies you in rows along both sides of your roads,
grows in the courtyard at home,
takes in
your native birds
as it interlaces breezes and the drone of locusts
like a hammock
for your siesta.

# Catherine Daly

## Howrah Bridge: Rabindra Setu

I drew in to Howrah Station along the river
to the city rising from the swamp.
Amid the muck and refugees, I saw a white bridge
cantilevered over the flat land and flat water,
improbable technology,
truss and girder like buttress and clerestory arch
spanning the Hooghly, thrust
into Calcutta. The bridge
is a new mathematical prayer
performed by clerks and reams of carbon paper,
clocked and numbered as if doves
fly across daily at 2:00 p.m.
Horse carts and chickens wander over its asphalt.

# Rubén Darío
*Translated from the Spanish by Greg Simon & Steven F. White*

## *fragment from* Santa Elena De Montenegro

Through smoky fumes of sulfur,
that stalking, medieval hunger ...
Oh, the smell of death! Oh, the horror!

Barking with a furious envy
the Devil's mongrels attack the sky
while the Mongibelo flows on by.

Whole cities tremble, delirious
from hunger, cold, and the fear of this ...
Oh, Jesus! Oh, Jesus! Oh, Jesus!

Dante's hair, in his Commedia's
pages, stood on end at the sieges
of the terrors of the Middle Ages.

Furies pass by, angers exploding ...
A thousand faces decomposing ...
Mournful omens the sky's imposing ...

A throng of ghastly human specters
who are gnawing at their own fingers …
The worms are adding to their oeuvres.

If the shrill trumpet at last falls silent,
what's creaking in the ears of the poets?
The bleak ossuaries of this planet.

# Gonçalves Dias
*Translated from the Portuguese by Greg Simon*

## SONG OF EXILE

My country has grown palm trees
in which the *sabia* sings.
Here, songbirds are not as sweet,
no, not here, not anywhere.

Our skies have more stars,
our meadows more flowers,
our woods have more life,
and our lives more love.

Alone at night, while I think—
this thought brings me such pleasure:
My country has grown palm trees
in which the *sabia* sings.

My country has grown its joy,
grown its fond and absent things.
In deep thought—alone, at night—
this thought brings me such pleasure:
My country has grown palm trees
in which the *sabia* sings.

My soul will not return to heaven
until I leave this alien shore;
until I once more feel that pleasure
that I never have been given here;
until I once more see the palm trees
in which the *sabia* sings.

# Norman Dubie

## M's Last Notes for the Lacrimosa

A small sack of coins. The nearly
empty inkwell. Wolfgang's
fever is a chart of three staves
written for more voices.
The witnesses
being stoned on tall palettes in Jerusalem?
The rough chorus
of stone breakers listing
stale bread to the cathedrals' badly lit height.

The dove trapped in the Apse
reeking of kerosene. The maestro's groin
with powder in it. *Cold salami
and stewed onions
next to manuscript.*

In this room of the manuscript
the living are scribbling in half arcs
of completion the music
that is suggested by simple talk
and a landlady's streaming in peak for the passions
that can clear the throat of all palcum.

*Shits and giggles.* The silence that visits
after the music stops
and the quiet after the landlady's
struggling aloft are equally worthy

of thought. Four ships of giggling
and the sweet onion broth
from a wooden spoon
touches the lips of the composer—
the one lung
like a rich man's tent seems to be filling
with sun. And then
the darkest cloud imaginable ...
empty of wind and rain.
It's into
the lye-pips with him.
Again.

Again. Like an old dog's
hind leg scratching fleas off his skin. Yet,
again.

# There Is a Dream Dreaming Us
## for Thomas James

> *Every little chamber was one reed long from the gate to the roof of a chamber to the roof of another, and door against door.*
> *—found in a jar outside Cairo.*

We are seven virgins. Seven lamps.
Each with a different animal skin on our shoulders.
We had crowns made of black mulberry with the pyracantha,
Its white flowers in corymbs spotted with yellow fruit.
On my forehead, in charcoal, is the striking digit
Of an asp, and with all of this we were nearly nude.

The procession to the pyramid began at the pavilion
At the very edge of the thirteen acres that were sacred.
We walked ahead of everyone with our priest,
But we are the last to leave this world for the portico
And the first gallery which is dark and cold.

We stood on the terraced face of the pyramid witnessing
The long entrance of the King's family.
The queen carried a lamb made of papyrus: its eyes
Were rubies. The Queen's brother was dressed
In little rattles made of clay.
Even the King's nursery followed him with two slaves
To the Chamber where we would all stay.

The sun no longer touched us on the plateau. It was lost
Making the sand dunes beyond the cataract rise and fall
Like water rushing toward us.
The glass doll was smashed above the portico,
And the doors began to close! We were inside the galleries
Of sun and flour and our seven lamps guided us
To the underground chamber. We could no longer hear
The drums leaving the inner acre.
I am the initial lamp and so I broke the last bottles
And from the bottles sand poured:
This last gate had two flanking chambers full with sand
And on the sand was the weight of marble columns,
Columns that joined the limestone slab that was
The last seal lowering now as the sand spills
Into two fern boxes on the floor.

The children had all been smothered and washed in oils,
All of the family is poisoned.
They sprawl around the sarcophagus which is open.
The priest has stabbed my six companions—it is
A noise like a farmer testing river soil.
I'm to drain the cup of wine that the King's mother
Handed me before dying. I was the *first lamp*, but

This is my story. I spilled the wine down my leg
And pretended to faint away. The priest thinking everyone
Had crossed from this world stopped his prayer. He walked
To the girl with the third lamp.
He kissed my dead sister on the lips. He ripped the silk
From her breasts. And then he fell on her.
Her arms were limp, I imagine even as they would be
If she were alive doing this with him.

The heat must have been leaving her body. He finished
And turned to me: what I saw was the longest
Of the three members of an ankh, all red, and from it
Came a kind of clotted milk.
But his strength was leaving him visibly; he put his
Dagger in his neck and bled down his sleeve.
I don't understand. But now

I'm alone as I had planned.
I'm a girl who was favored in the market by the King.
I've eaten the grapes that the slaves carried in for him:
If someone breaks into this tomb in a future time how
Will they explain the dead having spit grape seeds
Onto a carpet that was scented with jasmine?
The arrogance of the living never had a better monument
Than in me. I am going to sleep
In a bed that was hammered out of gold for a boy
Who was Pharoah and King of Egypt. My father died free.
My mother died a slave, here, at this site after being
Whipped twice in a morning. In the name of Abraham

I have displaced a King. I picked him up
And put him in the corner, facing in and kneeling.
He would seem to be a punished child.
What he did? I will tell you; you will be told many
       times again:

He killed four thousand of my people
While they suffered the mystery of this mountain appearing
Where there was nothing but moving sands and wind!

# Joseph Duemer

## CLUTTER

It used to bother me,
all this junk around the house
& I was always trying
to arrange the ten thousand things
(round stone from the road, bottle
from the beach at La Push, carved
bird, glass dog, shells & pictures
of classmates whose names
I have long forgotten, feather, lock
of a lover's hair, postcards ...)
according to some system
I could never quite figure out—
some aesthetic order
that might snap
the whole unruly collection
into a single word holding
in its strict syllabic tension all
the other words. Some magical
invented language dulcet
as birdsong. Some kind of dance.
Oh, I suppose you could say
I was looking for God
(or at least his reflection in a window)
though I didn't know it at the time
& would have denied it
if I had known.

("Why are you so angry at God,"
a woman asked me once. "Every boy
must hate his stepfather," I'd said.)
Or I just wanted to
make everything into a poem—
another false start, that.
Not everything here is sacred,
though a few missing
objects (the yellow piece of quartz
from the flank of Mt. Index
I lost decades ago …)
are numinous. That is, they glow
in the blacklight of memory.
(Those are the dearest.)
So I don't mind the clutter
the way I used to—Still, sacred
or profane, a lot of this crap
needs to go. It's beginning to stick
to me like the burrs the dogs
pick up in the woods.
I can't spend the rest of my life
picking them out of my fur.

# Simon Peter Eggertsen

## Twelve Questions in One Long Sentence

I have smelled the perfume of a thousand tonca beans hovering in the night air just above the forest path, and wondered what they could possibly add to the bitter taste of the cocoa, heard the paired green parrots chattering in the afternoon as they fly against the blue sky, and wondered what they were saying to each other and how long they would fly, waited for the crimson red of the ginger lilies to appear in the corner of the back yard, and wondered what pain provoked their deep, confused color, tasted the sense of the cherry-coconut ice cream, and wondered how to thank who ever thought of the mix, watched the yellow poui bloom all across the hillside, and wondered when the cooling rains would come, kissed the bites on my arm torn by the thorny branches of the red-purple bougainvillea along the driveway, and wondered who appointed them guard-dog sentinels, sucked on the rich yellow-orange flesh of the julie mango, and wondered how they got to be so sweet, opened the coconut and drunk its opaque water, and wondered where it got its coolness, danced the full brown cocoa beans around the box, oiling them up carefully for the 100-kilo bag, and wondered how many it would take to make a Hershey's Kiss, stripped the meager white flesh from the cocorite seed, and wondered how long it took to grow so little, healed the razor tears on my hand from the blade of a sharpened cutlass, and wondered how stupid I could be to blindly take it from the dark interior of the black knap sack, leaned toward the double rainbows over the Northern Range, and wondered who painted and hung them there?

# Paul Éluard
*Translated from the French by Peter Robertson*

## An Apologia for Knowledge VI

That night the most credulous eyes
would deny to the point of futility,
that night with nothing left to cling to,
the solitary stare impaled on the blot of ink.

## Closer to Us

Run, run to deliverance
and you will find that all is there,
and gather up its infinite wealth,
running so fast the cord will snap
at the sound a huge bird makes as it soars
into the ether, the flag a speck.

# Skip Fox

## Whatever Thing Death Be

pillow of desiccated flies as an emblem of silence, echo-less echoes of shadows tangled in shades gone down long halls of dreamerless dreams, tireless, streets and visions in a language of clouds, lost beyond founding?, or mind's certain peace wherein the walls of all its senses fall back and away, waking from fevered dreams, clear and weak, stinking, but a shower and breakfast will begin to fix all that, life stripped of itself like the past and morning so sweet it could crack your nut? the shifting grammars of oblivion, or mind's peace?, a mass of vowels, liturgy of wordless worlds floating in sky's lost grammar, syntax as slippage 'til friction itself, much less purchase, directive, resolve, is figment of the imagination, all things passing thru all things?, what of its manner that might be known?

## Blood in Black and White

5:53 a.m with weather en français (Channel 3) says
it's going to rain through the end of the week, five
days ringing the changes, wind in the rigging, my
operation always "incomplete," I walk away stunned,
amazed, while slashing the upper scenes, the movie runs,
masts in dismay. En français, indeed. Fucking in a foreign
language for instance. I just want to see you again, says the blind
man. Plunging into horror of water falling. Days lost, nights
      beyond
intent. Arguments raking the sides of dolphins with toy-sized
spurs, yet sharp as ferrets' teeth. You can barely see them beneath
the many-sided darkness stuccoed with wraith light, rising
and falling from sight amid gusts as a ghastly strobe marks
their passing back into the storm-tosst seas as you approach, a lens,
thoughtless, yet pregnant with attention, a bell with fruit, you can
almost make out fine lines of blood that appear to be pulsing
from the multiple and intricate serrations along their sides, lightly
glazing their torsos until they plunge back into wave and foam,
disappearing all over again. An old movie, a scene from a recurrent
dream, or living the cinematic trope for an ancient and un-
considered insistence upon what does not exist in the face
of the booming rush of each day, hour. Blood becomes
us, the sea on which we bob, our season's flood, strands
of water falling from eave to trough beneath, ringing
with proto-syllables, plunging deeper each day.

# Suzanne Frischkorn

## Chrysalis

Hair tangles signal three weeks of work,
each knot grows with each day in bed.
Once a woman,
a wife, a mother—
now a captive of the house.
Tied and bound by sleep.

Taking a shower makes her sleepy.
Pulling bristles through her hair, too much work.
As dirty dishes seize the house,
she scouts sheets and pillows on the bed
for misplaced anger at her mother.
Tired of being a woman,

she wonders if the title wears out all women,
if females need more sleep.
She decides to take a nap, then be a mother.
'Those synapses take a lot of work,'
she sighs and returns to bed.
Light retreats from the house.

She wants to be alone in the house,
resents that she's a woman
who's expected to get out of bed.
It doesn't matter that death and sleep
share the same job, do the same work.
Guilt hovers over this mother,

who refuses to speak to her own mother.
She feels safe in the house
it's the only talisman that works.
Makes her forget she used to be a woman
who never needed sleep,
and never stayed in bed.

"Hush. Sleep," croons the bed.
Her eyelids darken the role of mother.
Even a prince could not disturb this sleep.
Once rested she'll leave the house,
slip into the role of woman,
fix it so it works.

Soon the bed will not work,
and the woman becomes her mother,
even now, while she sleeps in the house.

# Tess Gallagher

## The Women of Auschwitz

were not treated so well as I.
I am haunted by their shorn heads,
their bodies more naked for this
as they stumble against each other
in those last black and white
moments of live footage.

Before she cuts the braid
Teresa twines the red ribbon
bordered with gold into my hair.
The scissors stutter against the thick
black hank of it, though for its part,
the hair is mute.

When it was done
to them they stood next to each other.
Maybe they leaned
into each others' necks afterwards. Or
simply gazed back with the incredulity
of their night-blooming souls.

Something silences us.
Even the scissors, yawing at
the anchor rope, can't find their sound.
They slip against years as if they were bone.

I recall an arm-thick rope I saw in China
made entirely of women's hair, used to anchor
a ship during some ancient war
when hemp was scarce.

At last the blades come together
like the beak of a metallic stork,
delivering me into my new form.
The braid end fresh and bloodless.
Preempting the inevitable,
Teresa uses the clippers to buzz off
the rest. Breath by plover-breath, hair
falls to my shoulders, onto the floor, onto
my feet left bare for this occasion.

As the skull comes forward,
as the ghost ship
of the cranium, floating
in its newborn ferocity, forces through,
we are in no doubt: the helm
of death and the helm of life
are the same, each craving light.

She sweeps the clippings onto the dustpan
and casts them from the deck
into the forest. Then, as if startled
awake, scrambles down the bank
to retrieve them, for something live
attaches to her sense of hair, after
a lifetime cutting it.

I am holding nothing back.
Besides hair, I will lose toenails, fingernails,
eyelashes and a breast, to the ministrations
of medicine. First you must make
the form, Setouchi San tells me, explaining
why the heads of Buddhist nuns are shaved.
The shape is choosing me, simplifying,
shaving me down to essentials,
and I go with it. Those women
of Auschwitz who couldn't choose—
Meanwhile the war plays out
in desert cities, the news shorn of images
of death and dismemberment.

I make visible the bare altar
of the skull.
Time is deepened. Space
more intimate than
I guessed. I run my hand over
the birth-moment I attend sixty years
after. I didn't know the women
would be so tender. Teresa takes my
photograph in Buddha Alcove, as if to prove
the passage has been safe. Holly, Jill, Dorothy,
Alice, Suzie, Chana, Debra, Molly and Hiromi offer flowers
and a hummingbird pendant, letting me know
they are with me. My sister
is there and Rijl.

*In Like Company*

I feel strangely gentled, glimpsing
myself in the mirror, the artifact
of a country's lost humility.
My moon-smile, strange and far,
refuses to belong to the cruelties
of ongoing war. I am like a madwoman
who has been caught eating pearls—softly radiant,
about to illuminate a vast savanna, ready
to work a miracle with everything left to her.

## Let's Store These Hours
### for Jim Fisher

Let's store these hours
while you are with us, but not
like a memory that says something
important is over and we have to
look over our shoulders to figure out
what. No, let's store the preciousness
of your presence in our own blood and breath
so when we step, you step and we never

get to any future which puts even one of us
out of sight. Let's take hands just to make sure.
And if anybody stumbles, we'll all stumble
onto our knees like a sudden joint prayer.
You're cracking jokes the whole time
like always because *always* is a safety zone
you carry us to when the health headlines
undermine the candelabra of the moment.

Come into our ancient cave of delight
and let us scrawl onto your heart the graffiti
of the angels who favor bison and deer—
those earth signs by which any future
welcome might embrace you as tenderly
as we do, because we are helpless with you
to hold back the days and hours
sweeping over us like a magician's cape.

*In Like Company*

You let us be helpless together—which
is a special kind of gift that takes down
the night sky, like a woman taking in her wash
at dawn, spilling starlight from shirt tails
and sleeves, into the dew-struck grass. For
that you will never leave us. For that

these words turn up their palms in supplication
and innocence. And to receive, as the sea-air of words do,
every nuance of your only-ness among us.

# John Gilgun

## Cold Morning

And white snow on the smooth cedar planks of the deck.
My voice has been stolen but the snow is singing for me.
It is singing a song about the olla, the Mexican stew-pot,
a mournful song about a snow flake which fell into the pot
and melted with the chicken, ham, carrots and onions.
I can see the clay pot and the body is streaked with soot
but the red rim shines in the light of a Mexican morning.
Smoke goes up from the firewood, la leña, consuming
itself to good purpose under the pot, which is enormous,
like a pregnant belly or the wrecked bus I saw once lying
on its side halfway down a mountain near Montemorelos.
And three crows sitting in silence on the crushed, rusting
roof of the bus and each one a prophet but none able to speak
because a curse has been laid upon them by the local bruja.
No point in asking them, "Who has stolen my voice and
how can I get it back? And when, when will I sing again?"

# Larry Goodell

## GODDESS OF THE BIG BANG

Beautiful as specimens of dust
under the microscope of your unaided eye
or the advanced stained glass windows
in the cathedral of the origin of mankind
dedicated to the Goddess of the Big Band
forever we come up like froth like filigree
    like delicate strands of DNA
in constant release of the first rising of the curtain
welcome what you're about to see
   is what you're about to see
what you're about
there's no ending to the play of fabricating nature
   fabricating itself from its own inner style
we are characters in surprise
   including our neighbors, every plant and animal
and hidden creature alive in the energy of the question,
we all want to live, audience and actors past in
   the present ever presenting itself
it's like love all around you and in and out you
   through and above seen in the spotlight
trained on every living thing Welcome
   to the mystery of the unknown
which is so obvious
you've known it all along.

# David Graham

## Heaven Changes

> *Sure, you might find him up at three*
> *But if he is it's just to pee*
> —Loudon Wainwright III

How when young we spoke
in the morning of party antics
the night before, who said and did
and how much and what and oh no,

but these days it's how well
or ill we slept, the grail being
seven or even eight straight hours
with no bathroom shuffle-dance

or existential vagueness for an hour
after three, and of course waking
at all, good heavens, and stepping
down on rug with minimal pain,

yes, heaven changes as you approach,
like a rainbow glistening in a field
toward which the young girl
gallops in joy of first touching

such magic, while we, who may
or may not have slept soundly
last night, watch her running
with noncommittal smiles,

in fact watching for that moment
we know is coming, when
the rainbow in all its glory
just vanishes, gone in a blink,


and there she stands, breathless
in the middle of a rain-dazzled
hay field, looking around and around
for wherever it could have gone.

# John Haines

## Watching The Fire II

Red bones of red men
are sleeping
in smoke and earth.

The fire is full of spears,
and dusty bonnets
that go up with a roar.

No one is awake
in the drafty camp of the dead.
No one is singing.

But a steady murmur,
and a thousand glowing eyes
still watch the night.

The fire is fed with fat,
with entrails and hair,
marrow of the great ox

whose black shoulders
carried the sun.
The men who killed him

*In Like Company*

came smeared with his blood
to make a bed of fire-stones,
to snore and to sleep.

Their bones are piled
in a vast and windy forest,
waiting for dawn.

# H. Palmer Hall

## The Car Hop at Sonic

It was not so much that I wanted
to run away, wanted to be with her,
but the waitress at Sonic, balanced
on her roller skates and almost

teetering backwards with the weight
of the tray, had somehow managed
to catch my attention. We flirted
through my open car window and

she said she got off at twelve and
wouldn't I want to get off, too, and
so, at twelve, I circled the parking lot,
looked at each menu with its speaker

attached and waited for an unbalanced
car hop, thinking this is just SO
fifties. When she got in my car, her
skates left behind in the glassed in

office, she seemed so much shorter,
her legs somewhat chubbier. Whatcha
wanna do? she asked and I quite honestly
did not know. I mean I had had some idea,

some notion of a cheap motel, some noir
fantasy of this and that, but the roller
skates had been a part of the scene. Her
mouth tasted of bubble gum. Perhaps

that was it. Or she no longer seemed
quite old enough for the cigarette she lit
when she got into the car. Or maybe
it was the flipflops on her feet, the pink

plastic purse, the iPod or ... so many things.
Everything seemed so common, nothing
like the Grand Hotel or Marlene Dietrich
or Grand Liaison ... just young and cheap.

# Ed Harkness

## Transitioning

For example, beads of rain
hang on the tips of pine needles,
each drop a clear, light-filled world.

On the other hand, clouds have the look
of an unmade bed, sheets wadded,
kicked into a corner of eternity.

Moreover, it's not surprising to find
I can't think of anything else
to say about the rain.

However, it leads to reflection.
Dodging a puddle, I catch in its flawed glass
the face of a man somewhat haggard,

frowning, an obvious introvert,
the soiled laundry of the sky
tumbling behind his head.

Furthermore, he is hatless. Weather, it appears,
is not his concern, just as baseball
is not the concern of thirteenth century monks.

Nevertheless, he sees himself passing
through one of those corridors of time
called Wednesday afternoon.

*In Like Company*

He hopes, additionally, this corridor
leads to one called Thursday, hopes, incidentally,
that he will not die, as Vallejo did,

on a Thursday, in Paris, in hard dirty rain.
Not die, in other words,
in the corridor of some other world

and its indescribable doors, each one
opening to more rooms than there are stars.
In sum, all things are connected,

just as trains transition to stations.
Thus, train bells; *ergo*, brain cells.
He, contrariwise,

looks up from his puddle, tosses French fries
to the shrieking gulls by the port
and, likewise, waits for his ship to come in.

# Charles O. Hartman

## Puddle System

The puddle gazes
at the sky, the sky
stares at itself in the puddle's
surface.
         To every season of reproach
its adequate gesture.
Blood floods an organ
such as the skin
and everyone raises
an eyebrow. Suitable
returns.
         A mother is gold, a father
a mirror. A man's ideal
is a close shave
but any miss good as a mile
bests a kilometer. Boys not only
will be boys, they are. A bad workman
blames his tool. In the end
every day turns out to be
a night. Only the neocortex
cares till it happens.

                    Distance they say
imparts enchantment
on loan, but anything
entering this mill is grist.
A man who plants trees
loves other and
later persons.
                    These figures
worked themselves out without
an Internet, as if someone
looked straight down through me.

# Jim Heavily

## Sonnets for Two Women

A calm desperation settles over the abandoned
Airstrip, nettled in its disuse & overgrown. You bring
Gifts & offerings, baskets of pumpkin
Seeds, chrysanthemums, radishes sculpted in a language
From another land; vials of antediluvial dust
& spices from the islands of Malacca, transfigured
Grape leaves, quiescent song birds arrayed on the fronds
Of anthologized palm trees, the day weepily
Slumbering as I reach for a last cigarette.
Sundown & comets. Hazy dawns & picnic tables.
The chimerical gift of your body, its darkest
Secrets & joys as if you knew, wanting to parcel
Out your adumbrated abundance, the heady
Scent of your heated, wanting body.

*In Like Company*

\* \* \*

The sun is setting & soon these warm bones
Will grow cold. Hilltops in the darkening
Foothills to the west breathe new life into
Rich earth, but not these bones.
There will be no new awakening
In spring. Nor will the river, flush
With an early thaw coursing over gold
Stones, rushing headlong oceanward,
Nourish this marrow. Aligned along
The wobbling pivot, true north shifting
With every passing age, there is only this:
We join those who've gone before & hope
That those we leave behind remember.

# Bob Herz

## Winner Take All

Past too bright landscapes of drugstores & car marts,
& the grand superchains beyond, & city parks,
Mendacious & leaf-choked, no place to stop unarmed,
& shoebox churches, tenacious on corner lots,
& mortuaries, closed banks, & post offices, the only traffic
A lone green paleo Pontiac rounding a corner,
Heading home, all fins & ghosts in tinted windows,
Wondering if in the valley, there was comfort, friends
To guide you, meet & praise you, but no, I thought,
No, that's not it.

The sudden rain ended & through parted clouds
Came sudden moonlight, & then wind's long sighs,
Strong, weak, then strong again:
Deceptive cycles, like a sick man's final days,
Signaling weather's local randomness
But really the smallest part of the larger pattern—
A lesson there perhaps, to gather in & hold, but no, I thought,
No, that's not it.

I walked angry on through the long long night
Scuffling finally slowing as exhaustion settled in,
But bringing none of the calm I sought, no
Nor surrender, but an enclosed thing,
Like a small truth hiding a larger lie, or the way
One lie hides & protects another, & hope hides all
& came then of a sudden with no holding back
Tears streaming raw & banal questions asked
As if to no one, to clouds perhaps or wet roads
In a world shrunken by the sad arithmetic of loss:
You, my friend, ten years senior, never now that
Long aging dignified familiarity I'd expected,
& seeing how wrong how childish a delusion,
Yes, I thought, this is it:

For I saw through finally to the ugly knowledge:
That aging is no small series of skirmishes, won or lost
Amid moments of grace, respites & speeches;
No, that's not it—it's a war, with a final loss
So absolute that the loser loses everything,
Life & friends & family & breath, & the winner takes all.
That's the secret of dying.  I learned it from you.
It's why I wept as I walked & could not stop walking
& hated myself for ever asking.

# Dennis Hinrichsen

## Living in the Other World

A man did not want to live
on the earth anymore.
Of course, I was partly responsible.
I made his nose larger than it really was.
I made him go without shoes
and it was cold!
I gave him stomach cramps.
He was opposed to this indignity,
this moral disgrace,
But what could I do?
I returned his nose
to its normal dimensions.
I made it warm.
So much for that.
But then dogs appeared.
Then the elms sprang up like doors
beside the creek
and spread out their plush umbrellas.
What's this? he asked.
I told him I didn't know.
If there is another world
then it must be like this one.
The shiny animals that appeared were crows.
The ones that had trouble walking
were about to fly.
At any moment they were
likely to cry out.

*In Like Company*

The other squat creatures were hens.
They would sift through anything for feed—
the man's toes, his children's toes,
his prize fields.
Was he happy now? He couldn't say.
I told him he should adopt certain habits
so we could not forget him.
I told him he should pronounce words
with a boorish flair
and we would love him more.
He sat down and lit up
a hand-rolled smoke the way
we have grown to love, if not imitate.
He gazed at his glorious elms.
They were black: it was snowing.
Those black trees were oaks.
Those black trees were oaks.

# Cynthia Hogue

## "THE GOOD"
### from *In June, the Labyrinth*

The cumulation of experience sufficient
to change heart
is the distinction between discovering
a space one has made,
a being one became,
and having refused. You reached
for moral limits to exceed them,
a "finisterre," a cliff:

if you leapt, were you more
or less moral? You loved from afar,
way, way from the bottom
of your heart, that sheer
drop down, down, you'd fallen
in love. Then space estranged.
The strangeness could not—
there was nothing you could do—

grow familiar again. Now no time's
left to try something else, something
other than, though new perceptions
intervene, complicate what is simply
the essential morality of goodness:
*Are you a* good *woman*,
you're asked by a stranger, alone,
at breakfast in a little *pensione*.

*In Like Company*

You, speaking truth to
an intruder on your solitude
(*I* try *to be*), surprised by

the force of the kiss, fight, win:
being close enough to touch
differed from your distant love,
safely abstracted from presence.
Your goodness found in the forgiving.

# Christopher Howell

## Flood

### I.

Even in our sleep we hear it, the roar of everything
and nothing much
passing over us like Fortune and Justice drunk
laughing it up in the bar next door, pig iron loads
of unanswerable prayer and imprecation
stuck to their large old shoes.

### II.

*Caution! Stay Where You Are! Please Leave
Your Payment in the Blood Red Cup.*

Dear son, come home, we've decided to spare the dog
and hang you.

One step at a time now. You can *make* it. The water
is not *that* deep.

III.

We're out of sugar and we're out of light. Someone
keeps saying there is a giant assigned to each of us,
that you can hear them wading, seeking us out
in our nailed shut rooms below the stairs.

One of the giants keeps saying he loves us all, he really does.
And the others trust him, see, though he's nothing
but a whisper in the hard dark
beside us,

though he's a woman, too, or the mink-soft touch
of an accident or a moon we didn't know was there
all along, shining
as though nothing in the world were wrong.

# Gray Jacobik

## The Power Outage

Still to be done, a few last Sunday night chores;
washed clothes to be folded and put away,
trash to go out. Simple doingness,
the respite of tasks. Bats are grazing fields
of air, a hoot owl calls in the back woods.
Visible from an upstairs window, the cloud-caught
glow of an end-of-summer carnival goes
suddenly black as all else. Must be children
caught on the Ferris wheel. Palms slide down
banisters to the candle drawer. Nothing to do
but go to bed. The world is as dark as it ever was.
Wind is awash in the music of trees. We rest
in one another's arms but there's no spark
between us tonight, nothing to kindle,
so I voice a memory and you voice another,
and we go back and forth like this, surveying
in deep enclosing darkness, the turns
circumstance and promises have given us.
We seem to be drifting together everywhere
and nowhere at once, then the old impression
of eternity sneaks up, that vivid mercurial
feeling of before and now and again and yes
love, you, and yes love, me—somehow, forever,
we're sure of it. Or perhaps this is only human,
unable as we are to imagine not being, or an end
to our love, the sense of a saving, needed haven,
ours when light has failed and we're in the dark.

# Laura Jensen

## My Father At Times

My father at times would say aloud
out of the quiet alive light
that was our house
he would say, as though it was
after a hesitation, he would say, oh—

and no one would say anything.
Then he would continue.
He would say my mother's name
and then the sentence that followed

would be about something he remembered
or about something that needed to be done
or about something he had just read in the paper.

And she would answer him.

## A Poem and What a Poem Has Become

At a long yard, a set-back small old house
three or four steps up from the sidewalk
there is a poem and what a poem has become.

On the short bank there is a chainsaw eagle.
On the short knotted grass of the bank, by the sidewalk
There is a cobweb draped across the lower part.

The eagle's face looks down and to its left.
And this is like a crucifix. One wing
shows yellow at a seam where once it was glued on.

One half of the base is torn. The day is overcast.
Other yard sale remnants with it are uneven and few.
The six-lane traffic goes past relentlessly.

# Halvard Johnson

## Schattenwelt

*Contra mundum*—yes, well, weren't we all
in those days. A thick shake, along with fries
and a burger, was enough to get us out
on the streets, agitating, waving placards,

daring the pigs to come get us. We'd argue
until dawn, then a half-hour nap before
going to work, eyes red and brains glazed
over. Please don't get me wrong, I've never

misused the workplace for my own ends.
High-octane memories cloud my views
of reality. You know, I know you do.
The part of my brain for solving ethical

problems has long been off-limits to any-
one with anything to sell, rent, or lease.

# Jesse Lee Kercheval

## Japanese Expedition to Antarctica, 1911–1912

> "This film premiered in Tokyo in 1912. The expedition leader, Lieutenant Shirase, later used the film many times while lecturing."
>
> *Le Giornate del Cinema Muto* catalogue, 20th edition

1120 feet of film
of the Shirase expedition
& all I remember is this—
Japanese in fur-lined parkas
tipping over penguins,

as if they were bowling pins,

as if they were cows, back home in Wisconsin.

# Federico García Lorca
### *Translated by Greg Simon*

## WIDOW OF THE MOON

Widow of the moon—
who could forget her?
She dreamed the earth
turned into crystal.

Furious and pale,
she hoped to sing the sea
to sleep, comb her hair
with cries of coral.

Her hair like spun glass—
who could forget it?
At her breast, the rims
of a hundred wells.

Tall jets of water
like battle-lances
guard her by the waves
of the tranquil dunes.

But the moon, the moon—
when will it return?
The curtains of wind
flutter ceaselessly.

Widow of the moon—
who could forget her?
She dreamed the earth
turned into crystal.

And you, Count Arnaldo,
how could we forget
your dream of the earth?
Crystal, all crystal.

# John Morgan

## A Renaissance Altarpiece

Uccello painted them: a family bound
together to a tree-trunk post, staring
with horror down as flames leap up from
foot to calf to knee. Four horsemen on
the right display the flag of Rome. Across
from them, with faces glistening in the flame-
light, stand the helmeted guards who
trussed this family up and set them blazing.

Two boys, both red-heads, share their parents'
fate, while in the background—fields, a leafy
apple tree, farm houses, and a church.
The sky behind a neighbor castle town
is black. The merchant and his pregnant wife
and boys were damned for what they did to
*desecrate the host*. "Religion," I once
told a Catholic friend, "makes good people better,

bad people worse." Another panel illustrates
their crime. They cooked it in a pan until
it bled. The blood of Christ spilled out and ran
across the floor, and when it dribbled
underneath the door, they were exposed.
Have you ever fallen from the second
story window of a dream—the broken
glass, the silent floating scream? You'd think

at least the child in her womb could be
redeemed. Why would a Jewish merchant
be so hostile to the host? Why in
Urbino was this credited? What calculus
of feeling can elucidate this art, unless

it charts a program to annihilate
a race. Aghast, the baffled victims
stare at lizard flames that leap and leap.

# Peter Munro

## Elegy For What Falls

Wringing the first hints of crimson from each leaf,
a northerly strikes the maple, a timbrel
singing in a tempo more relentless than grief.

Winged seeds flutter, sail up in a whirl. No prayer
rises as gracefully. The whole earth trembles
as the seeds crash to soil and ruddy leaves flare.

Toadstools breach detritus, surfacing to air
gills burdened by spores. They nudge tiny temblors,
rippling a rhythm more ancient than despair.

My insignificance comforts me. I tell
the news: a sparrow falls like a seed. Tumbled
through bell-clear air, its ringing feathers dispel,

attenuating in an empty temple.
Let the maple bleed until its leaves crumple.

# Sheila Murphy

## Lauds (11)

Allow the meantime rain to wash this habitat and circumstance
Made blond by morning so that we might parse secular
    dividends
And allocate uneven heart light as if to have been indisposed
Would guarantee transfer-of-sadness into a routine
That turns to maturation of each undiscovered miracle
Before receding into a reciprocal delicion

When I talk to you I hear anti-depressant slivers
Take down your voice so its incessant melody
Begins to lie still as a sacrament and I have something
To worship all over
Again alongside lifetimes of reflexive architectural
Hovering

Why can't we photograph the future, that we might
Learn what to keep before it has arrived and gone
To seed like most offspring and the very thought of them
Becoming duplicative memories on the very cusp
Of dismay before it gets out
That warm waves we used to think about
Could spoil a season leaving us
Little to eat too much to earn and nonexistent places
We might walk and learn and pluck habitual sacrifice
Out of the life

# Pablo Neruda
*Translated by Greg Simon*

## Torrid Ode

Send me cargoes of red instructions,
summers all-scorching, the world's sourest fruit trees;
pack away my feelings under bags of sweat,
blind me with radiant light, with ancient lightning,
corrode my heart with searing coal or ceramic kisses,
slash into my intestines, ripping away
at my soft inner being like food that hungers for me,
peppers, chilies, ginger, mollusks, burnt walnuts,
food that tears at me like crabs and still
flows on, soil without end, slurry after slurry,
into my oddly irritated throat,
your gooey sources of sugar,
endless streams of sperm, O progenitor of earthly life,
sublime concoctions of oil, the urine of bestial savages,
the buffalo's end-of-the-world mud and rice paddy slush,
tea and monsoon rain and dew on the orchids,
earth of hellish reconciliations,
my sky;
blend my soul with your substances,
your exorbitant and stubborn soil,
your nourishing stones and still more:

your mineral roots, the skin and fur of your animals,
the claws and beaks of your tireless birds,
your demented instruments, the dark
noises, as disturbing as thunder in the sky,
your silence, languid and lively, like alcohol or acid,
and the secret numbers of death and longevity
buried in the ordinary earth of my soul.

# Sergio Ortiz

## Only the Rumor

I, who have rarely seen sanity,
or a caravan of Siberian huskies stroll
with their pack through soft white snow,
have no appreciation for winter's twilight-silence,
or the ruckus of grizzlies ravaging
my provisions.

I ask: Is there anyone
willing to put their hand in place of mine
on the chopping block, or their signature
on paper to demand investigations
into all that has been stolen
on my passage through this life?

I have not seen tenderness
nor do I feel excitement upon observing
the child fed from the safety of its mother's hands.
Only the rumors of the existence of distant cities
where harsh winters outlast serene summers
accelerate the rhythm of my blood.
That chill is mine.

I, who have rarely seen reason, have played
with water and snow. I've wrapped them around
my legs, given them form with my hands like a lover.
I, who am fed-up with listening to wolves
and sleeping under willows, no longer tremble
when they throw down my door to take me
where neither water nor snow exists.
Do you understand? It is nothing more

than a short visit to the crying room
of a psychiatric hospital, a show

to impress the animal
that sleeps beneath
the sheets.

# Sam Pereira

## The Blue Scent Of Juniper
*for Susan*

Wisteria were called for here. He knew that. He crawled
And spat into a sink and shaved. He doubted the Church
On a daily basis and he drank until his skin gave
Off the blue scent of juniper and ice. She took form
Over years: a slow shadow enveloping the evenings.
He had thought about her ultimatums; their history
And pomp. She had saved his life and it wasn't that
At all. Cars raced underneath his building. Kids screamed over
Whatever this particular morning's good game happened to be.
She'd washed his soul with tears. He'd dried her
With the tail of a dark shirt, taking it off in one quick stroke.
It was Friday. He remembered getting lost
On a bus for her. She laughed and cringed, knowing
More would be expected later. He accepted, though.
It was the most important acceptance in his witless career.
Roses were called for then. The most magnificent the streets
    offered.
These gifts were small. He knew that. Dropped into the water
    glass
Of a better than average hotel, things took on a kind of silver
    glint, unseen
On either coast for decades. He knew that and he shook. With
    each year,
The flowers changed. Lately, the sun had taken on the color
Of dandelions floating on his imagined lake. While this image
    jostled,

Reflected next to a gathering of ducks and a crushed paper cup,
He remembered that everything floats for moments. He
    remembered
The chocolate rhythms of breathing in winter. He remembered
    a book and
The two people in it and how the man had the good sense to die.
Ice-carved peonies would do well here, placed strategically,
On top of his chest where, he'd once blurted out in all certainty,
    no
One would ever rest their head but her. Peonies should be
    remembered
Like birthdays. Some said he smiled and waved one time and
    was gone.

# Method

In the years I've known you,
You have always been
The one to traipse
Into the moonlight,
Wearing only a necklace
And a smile. I like
That about you.
The necklace usually reflects
The lake-like shimmer
In your eyes, or
The hot pink lacquer
Adorning those charming feet.
Let's say I'm in love with you.
Every twig I step on
Magically repeats your name.
It's bad drama, but it's ours.
Sure, I'm in love with you,
And this becomes my final
Chance at convincing you.
Are you ready? Take off
Your necklace quickly now,
And make love to me
Before the film crews show up
To take shots they will turn
Into posters for every theater
Across the contiguous universe.
Right there. That's it. Kiss me
Slowly, into the applause.

# Ignacio Ruiz Perez
*Translated from the Spanish by Carlos Reyes*

## Self-Portrait Of Coleridge

He draws his insolent face:
a sepia image
and the curved line of his nose.
The wickedness that changes
dawn strips his
thoughts bare.
He sketches a smile:
a pair of gulls,
three bearded fish,
and an old sailor
sink slowly into his eyes.

## Billy Budd Enchained

There is nothing left but travel
see the deserted islands
hoist anchors
listen to songs of the sirens
tie myself to the mast
and scan the western horizon....
The passage of time doesn't frighten me:
the gasping fish tied to starboard
scares me more.
Looking at his teeth,
I think of the morning: opening
beneath the lens of a microscope,
approaching the poisonous frogs
that will likely be put
on my tongue
to keep me from speaking
the language of the waves.

# Doug Ramspeck

## Tupelos

What trance they must have fallen
    into. The ovoid blue-black
fruit dangling as a strange sadness
    in the dusk light. The gray
bark furrowed into alligator hide.
    The leaves dreaming like fence slats
as the wind goes rushing through them,
    like moths transfixed and bumping
at the porch light, as though it is possible
    for photons to coalesce and know
each other as the sum of their amplitudes,
    in the intimacy of their quantum physics,
like water flowing into water across
    the broken rocks of the river
beyond the trees.

They are long married, our tupelos,
    which we can tell by the way the names
sound against the tongue—blackgum, pepperidge,
    beetlebung, sourgum. And by the way
the elliptical leaves lean all in one direction—
    at the same time as the trunks turn
subtly away from one another, as though
    they have grown so far from the soil

they can't go back. As though they have pledged
 themselves only to the tallest canopy
of leaves, which take the long view,
 which rise even higher than our house
and follow the river until it disappears
 beyond the ridge.

Or maybe not sadness but a weathered
 isolation, the pith chambered as partitions,
the decaying holes where the small animals
 hide, the outstretched limbs
where once we saw the starlings alight
 in their green glossy multitudes, the branches
bending beneath the weight of the abundance.

# Rochelle Ratner

## STEPS

Having decided the casket will be a perfect fit, the small red velvet pillow under her head more than comfortable, she gets up and begins again. This time she'll let him in. Except, guiding him toward where her heart should be, her breast is but another unexpected obstacle. Okay, breast then. Fresh, healthy, mint-green breast, just a faint odor of cow dung. It will aid the growth, they say. It's crowded but, little hangman stick figure that he is, she can fit him in. She never was much good at drawing. Cute little man with bowler hat and toes pointed up, she feels his rubber soles moving about, tentative at first. Finally, a heartbeat.

# Carlos Reyes

## The Snake

The gauze-like ghost
of a two-meter-long
snake rustles in the light breeze
along the dusty road.

On close examination
I see the husk of that reptile
is still stuck to the hole

in the wall it has forced
its way through
to be reborn.

On the other side,
in a shiny new coat
it is blind to the world
as any new kitten.

When its vision clears
it will go searching
for a new life.

Reminds me
I have often crawled
through holes
of grim stone walls, trying

to leave more
than my old rain coat behind, hoping

the wind would blow it away
and with it all my sins.

I am not trying
to be anthropomorphic,
I am not a snake, it is that simple.

On the underside
of the sloughed skin
I examine
perfectly imprinted ridges:
the snake's means of travel—

I look at my own worn shoes.

# Tad Richards

## EVOLUTION

Music came first, an unbroken pure tone
passing over the smooth surface of clay, how long
no way to count, until ripples
ridged the clay, and the music found them
and began to rise and fall, billions and billions
of times (call them years), until buds
extended, became digits, pushing
up from the clay, wriggling,
swaying side to side, all moving together,
a metronome, marking the rising
and falling tones, billions upon billions,
highs growing infinitesimally
further from lows. Then four
fingers, as they had become, held back
behind the tone, waved response
to another four, neither a hand yet.

The waving fingers began to break
ranks, waggle to each other. New patterns
made for shifting air currents; the tones changed,
more rapidly now, a million years, now half
a million, more, less, with rapid
irregularity, and the second group
of fingers began to tap the clay
they had sprung from. The tones absorbed the taps
for a while, then moved with them,
propelled by them, pushed this way and that,

and rhythms came into the void,
four fingers tapping, four dancing,
contrapuntal, infinite variety
which needs nothing more than itself, and could have
gone on forever, but that the fingers
pushed further out of the clay, a new nub appeared,
became a thumb, and pushed against the fingers
sounding a snap in air: a beat.

The dancing fingers loved
the beat; they moved with it,
around it, against it. Mostly,
it propelled them, they stretched upward,
pushing through clay, they became hands,
then wrists, then arms that jointed, and would have
jointed again, but that shoulders
grew out and stopped them.. But the beat
went on, and the hands were drawn
back to the clay, the music pulsed
around them, the notes were blue,
the rhythms syncopated, and this
was happening all over now, shoulders,
arms, hands from the clay,
back to it, and the clay growing soft
and malleable where the hands
and the music touched it. The hands
began modeling, some pulling it up,
and up, some making finger-width grooves, fingers
probing inside the grooves, until the music
and the hands and the new shapes
made the clay moist and fecund, and
algae grew, and sporangia.

# Mary Ruefle

## SUDDENLY

It's like there's more oxygen
in the air or something
or 107 baby's faces have been enlarged
and are drifting across the sky
I also saw a leaf-blower
and all the dead leaves
looked like they were having fun
jumping around as if they were alive again
I think too of a certain recipe
that calls for eelgrass
which the scallops love to swim in
And on top of it all
a profound sense of nothingness
has come into play
so I tell everyone I was born
at sea among the meadow people
who never speak a word
that has not been repeated
over and over and over again
but still takes me completely
and by surprise.

## All This, All This

All of art was invented
by the discontented.
A man in a black armband
filling a bowl with cereal.
A woman throwing a gray sweater
over a chair she's too exhausted
to sit in. They stand there,
watching the first sunrise
after my death. My god,
how beautiful orange can be.
Though it's made a little better
by purple.

# Jim Simmerman

## Tell The Truth

Whatever she said in bed to you was a lie,

or else, something she had already said,
in another bed, to somebody else.

Didn't it make you shiver nonetheless,

and blush in the dark like the digital clock?
Whatever she said in bed to you was a lie.

Though meant, perhaps, to draw you closer,

it set you adrift in thought, instead,
to somebody else, in another bed....

Whatever truth there was, was in the numbers

trading places on the face of the clock.
Whatever she said in bed to you was a lie

you already knew by heart. You'd heard it

before, said it yourself, in the dark,
to somebody else, in another bed.

The truth was in the numbers, and the numbers

were disconnected dots. Whatever she said
in bed to you, she was lying, like you,

in another bed with somebody else.

# Greg Simon

## Song [Self-Analysis]

after Fernando Pessoa

Every poet's a forger—
they'll fake whatever they can

including the pains I know
belong solely to poets.

Whoever reads their poetry
won't experience those pains,

just pain made of blue vapor
from stars we never knew fell.

As when—shunting aside all
awareness—the clockwork trams

we refer to as our hearts
roll along their iron rails.

# Song [The Slivers]
### *after Fernando Pessoa*

Not for me a picket fence
around the soul—that's for deaf,

blind and dumb ones! I need
to feel everything, all the time!

When I'm awake, I gaze down
at the earth and sky. Nothing

I see belongs to me. I say
that innocently! But it

doesn't mean the earth and sky
have no effect on me.

I watch them. I want to join them
so intensely. I can change!

I can splinter and disperse—
break my soul into pieces ...

into each well from which
the one who is whole must drink....

*In Like Company*

And if I can't examine
my soul the same way each time,

how dare I think I have
the right to say anything?

I can't even look inside
myself without flinching

because everything I've learned
has come to me in slivers!

How do I go on existing
when my soul goes off to hide?

In this I imitate the gods,
or one of them, who, in a flash

of pleasure, took the infinite
some place beyond its center.

# David Starkey

## THE INCREDULOUS MIDWIFE

Her friend and fellow midwife exclaims, *A virgin
has given birth to a son!*
                    But what fool
believes such a tale? She insists she must thrust
her finger inside and search the parts.

Since her good-for-nothing husband decamped,
she takes nothing on faith.

As she reaches down into the blood
and straw, her fingers curl up like a snail
retreating into its shell.
                    She wails
until a supercilious angel appears
above the manger—a middle manager
chastising a churlish copy boy.
                    *Hold
the child*, he commands. She does, of course,
although this early in the story—
the shed stinking faintly of shit,
the little assembly staring her down like a band
of outlaw musicians about to miss
its gig—
          God's forgiveness
hardly seems a certainty.

*In Like Company*

# The Healing of the Blind Man

As Jesus and his disciples troop
like a pack of feral dogs
up and down the dusty lanes of Jerusalem,
they pass a blind man sitting in the shade.
Simon Peter asks:
   *What sin did he commit,*
*master? Or what were his parents' sins?*

In answer, Jesus spits on the ground
and rubs the mud into the frightened man's eyes.
He recoils, but Jesus commands him
to wash in the pool of Siloam.
      Tapping
with his cane until he finds the water,
he splashes his leathery face—skin the color
of an avocado that's been left out overnight—
then stares out on the bright-lit chaos
for the first time.
         Surrounded by rubberneckers,
he makes his way into the newly
perceptible world, looking so happy
and oblivious, it's possible to imagine him
ages hence,
      driving a battered Volvo
fifty miles an hour in the fast lane of the freeway,
singing full-throated with the radio,
utterly ignoring the other drivers'
flashing headlights and honking horns.

# Pamela Stewart

## IF TRANSLATION

*is a doorway, a window, and the bridge*
*music makes across moving water, if*

a woman's last three dying breaths
are the steps she took her first day of school
and if twenty years later twirling
with her new husband across the church hall's
polished floor is applauded
by death's small smile from the corner
where the women with thick legs sit
and the skinny ankles of men with ribbed
black socks bob up and dawn
to the cheery sentimental tunes, then

*translation weaves over and under while time*
*shuttles back and forth from that first moment*
*before a moment can be understood*

# The Same Window

Mist rises to lavender behind that old shed
with its tiny metal chimney. From your kitchen
an old-timey tick-tock nudges minute to minute.

No point in daily news. Your country
rips tantrum to tantrum.
You know *you're* not dead yet, so who's left?

    You watch smoke lift behind the shed
where your neighbor has started a small fire.
*What's he up to now?*

Step by slow step you reach the steaming kettle,
then haul it to the table. A mug of coffee
and a little sit-down by the window begins the reckoning.

# Carolyn Stoloff

## Lorca's Silence

Lorca cuts his thumb on silence
I soak up his silence with my bread
His silence smells like sun on dust
Feels muscular as an eel
Looks like foam on the flanks
Of exhausted horses

When night's hard forehead
Presses against me
I smoke Lorca's silence
Through seams
In the house of his poem

# Lynn Strongin

## "The Magpie Is a Most Illustrious Bird"

—Donovan, "The Magpie"

*for Penelope*

> He said, "I want to hear all that's pretty,"
> He said, "I want to hear all that's nice."
> —Donovan, "The Mandolin Man and His Secret"

WERE THE SHOES WERE THE WINGS OF THE CHLD
*Lifting parachuting her forward in overalls holding baby*
  *into the summer day*
*by brightening knighting chidlhood*
*O all of them scrambled like wild men*


I.

SWEET FEET
              long tapered in my hands like gloved skin
speak for me who am paralyzed             in my pain
who once wore shoes that led into this photo of
        me holding baby, the way kids go tussling.

You have sweet feet
I notice        crossed at night stretched out sitting up
    in bed watching the sun circus.
One crossed over the other    yes after forty years
Most illustrious
All that's pretty
All that's nice
You coming home to me
Rag & bone man bedding down in charcoals
Your homecoming to me
Will suffice.


II.

CHILD WAKING IN NIGHT TERROR

She knows him        she does not know her child,
    shaking him, staring into coals aflame for olive eyes:
Food means love to him
Rhubarb pie
He stares motionless into space
He has the croup
She takes him into the parking lot
Gracefully illuminating challenges will come to him at age
    fourteen with luck
Medieval boy haircut
Bangs
Mystical
Like voice
Just incisively
Cut.

The fish loves water
But I hate parades
Because really what is there to célèbre?
I love raspberry autumn
But I the
Heat
Ice crème carnivals
Parades of dark nigh after dark night
Waking up in a sweat:
Mumm please quick dip me in water.


III.

Night Terrors in Children

What are we, baked potatoes?
His skin is taut          he stares at me          his mother
Who am I
Then screams seven minutes     filmed without unclosing
          his eyes once
I etch over the best of children & pray when
My time come
I fold both hands a dove
In away that would quiet him.

# Jeanie Thompson

## To Lesbos

*I. The Shell of the Hawksbill*

This harp won't warm into a song
For you or anyone, these strings

And our separation make things clearer.
They cloud the past like the tortoise-shell's

Milky reds, yellows, and browns.
Today I've walked for hours through cypresses

Tossed by a late summer wind.
I long for the stillness of olive groves

Heavy with fruit, a song for you,
My fingers barely touching the strings.

I would sing just for you.
How did I come so far from

Where once I walked out
Of an olive grove toward a marble cliff,

The air and sea open to me.
Below the sheer drop, I could see a girl

*In Like Company*

Gathering jonquils and anemone.
She chose blossoms for her hair

Bright as torchlight.
It was then I closed my eyes

And the wind became a voice
Carrying my song,

Pressing against her,
Molding the soft shapes of her tunic.

I imagined her translucent skin
Growing warm at this touch.

When the sun fell,
Like a coin dropped for luck into the Aegean,

I could believe in signs from heaven
As pure as the song rising from the warm sea

Touching a young girl        who knows nothing.

## II. Lotus

One I dreamed your mouth
Was the lotus flower opening in a kiss.
Your lips were pale petals
Tinged with silver.
As I brush my hair loose,
The feel of it lifting off my shoulders
With the night winds
Is like your hand, reaching to pull me back.
Tonight no one notices me walking alone
Along the shore.
Rocks lovingly bruise my bare feet.
Night opens on the marble cliffs, specters
Flicker, indistinct as the dead,
Gone when the creamy moon rises....

We lay on the bleached rock
And couldn't speak. My nightdress
Dampening on the beach.
You loosened the purple band
From my loop of hair.
Against your warm skin
The moon was a light breath.
When you came into me,
A song held the moon back.
I believed for that moment
She was benevolent, a mother
Covering us with soft, yellow light.

But tonight, beside the black pool
Of the sea, the moon seeps into my skin.
In a country as far away as death,
You walk to me forever on a rocky beach.
Your arms,
The limbs of an olive tree, lift me
To be kissed, but the moon's fragrant lips
Touch my eyes in sleep.
As you lower me slowly to the rocks
I take no notice
If they welcome me with small gifts,
Jewels of purple and black. I am joining you

Along Acheron, to watch the moist flower open.

## Marina Tsvetaeva
*Translated from the Russian by Alex Cigale*

\*\*\*

Into the blue sky, eyes open wide:
How I exclaim—Thunder will stride!

Passing a man I raise my brow:
How I exclaim—Still there is love!

Feeling beyond apathy's gray mist:
I still exclaim—There will be verse!

*1936*

\*\*\*

Your years are—a mountain,
Your time is—that of kings.
Fool! To love—you're too old.
Old friends mean—more than love.

Older than monsters, roots,
Older than altar's stone
On Crete, older even than
The oldest druid's runes.

*January 29, 1940*

\*\*\*

Two suns grow cold—spare me God please!
One—up in the sky, the other—in my breast.

Just as these suns—can I forgive myself?
Just as these suns had made me crazed!

And so they both chill—their rays cause pain.
The one that cools first had been the warmest.

*October 5, 1915*

\*\*\*

Fate arrives not with a roar or thunder
But just so: snow falls,
Street lamps glow. A man walks
Up to the door.

He raises his eyes and ascends the stair.
The long spark the doorbell expels.
In the house absolute silence,
And the figures on fire.

*November 16, 1916*

\*\*\*

It's time to shed my amber,

It's time to trade in words,

It's time to dim the light

Above my door....

*February 1941*

# Liliana Ursu
*Translated from the Romanian by the poet, Adam J. Sorkin and Tess Gallagher*

## THE SAND OF OLIMP

I am translating the poems of George Szirtes
on a skittish afternoon in early May.
Near my feet, a kitten, its eyes just opened,
wobbles its first steps.
The shadow of the flowering raspberry canes
creeps slowly along my leg
while somebody strides triumphantly
across my shadow,
somebody from the past.

On the white table in the garden, my eyeglasses,
a dictionary, Cavafy, The Bestiary of Helen Dunmore,
The Lives and Works of the Great Saints.

I open the big, brightly colored umbrella.
At the moment I translate the last lines,
about the accordion player and the blind intellectual,
with the closing phrase, "Be wise, be good."
Evening falls. I shut the umbrella.

Suddenly, everything is salted with fine sand,
touched by the beach and by the sea, wintered together
there in the folds of my umbrella.
Now they sift onto this May freshness,
over the finale of my day—ethereal, beatific,
as if an angel unfurled its wings.

## A Path to the Sea, or the Letter *A*

In the morning all things in their place:
first the heart, next the coffee
steaming in its white cup, the roses
baptized with dew from the May sky—
and now the shadow of a fleeting thought
which, for such a long time,
has been circling me.

Without a whisper it alights
on my welcoming page, like sand
to a shore scrubbed by the sea—one moment
enriched, the next
impoverished.

Freed of my life,
the poem takes my place
in the garden
near a small secret door
opening onto the sea.

All things in their place. Yet nothing
what it was.

# Roger Weingarten

## Self-Portrait as The Magnificent Frigatebird

This kleptoparasite, a.k.a. Man O'War, silent at sea, all darkness through under parts, head and back feathers: sunlit and fluffed into iridescence.

En route to Woman Key, sanctuary for shipwrecked whore, I swallow baby turtle climbing a thermal. Maybe I'll press my scarlet throat pouch against a white breast, upwind from coral reef. Aerial pirate, Messerschmitt, I force great birds to disgorge flying fish scrap.
Gathering: a reed in my straight hooked bill for mate number four to weave a frail nest archipelago

nights and days I peer into the wake of Triton's horses. Highjacker in the clear,
I never alight; I can't—weak-legged glider—dive through that ultramarine crust.
Frégate superbe, I slap my bent wings against talking drum of my red gular sac to beguile her.
Invertebrate-eater, I dip and snatch squid and jellyfish. Fregata
colonials vulnerable to attack steal mates, nesting materials, eggs and young. I,
Elvis impersonator reincarnated as magnificent—flow from grace, chipper softly, headshake side-to-side at

nesting ground—kack kack to attract another from wheeling overhead regatta. This Elvis knockoff abandons mate and half-grown chick to molt and breed with others. Fledgling number one wanted his mother to feed him until she dropped. Dare to forget: Rakish lines—ravenous, climbing heaven—that drop to forage drifting gulfweed for frogfish. In a mangrove cay off a coral reef, I, Lord Byron of Misrule, graceless dust devil in reverse, circle and dive to inhabit this roosting mysterium,

a wandering Jew zigzagging land's end from the Isle of Man to British Columbia toting bloodstained bagpipe, kept aloft by forked tail and pointed wing. Erect, I clack my bill to launch my strawberry inflated pouch's theatrical season. Barn swallow of the sea, I quiver, click, wheeze and grate to lure new mate. Ashkenazi, I flipped my little brother out the second story window into a flying ritual childhood motif. Rely on one egg to a clutch, rarely two. I

dream Barak asks me to pilot his run for a second term. I prefer, I text back, priapic erection or arsenic. Protected: but still killed in the nest with torches and clubs—some years no young survive. Marine oscillations over the Isthmus of Panama, caromed between six years and sixty-seven, Roger, are you pipedreaming a knife-toting bad guy floating mid-air? Are you your own Judas goat trotting out—for birdwatcher glued to spotting scope—your Sagittarius sun conjoined with Mercury the thief? Rolling over for Saturn in suspenders alias Dad in opposition might help adjust to being less. Father?

*In Like Company*

Am I forgetting a father's key ring charm: a lead shmuck paired with padlocked yoni? Is there a point ? Dead from brain cancer, shorn to the pink. Gulls laughing, wind luffing, the snake-haired stepmom for the ages shrieks, Why didn't you call your dying papa? Sphinx-faced Mom hurls ashtray at Dad. Skin of firstborn split. Entangled species—lost European tribe and Cleveland flock—in two places at once. Last shot over the bow for Xmas Island Frigatebird's fledglings polished off by yellow crazy ants. Honeycomb flight dream redux : soaring Escher stairs into thick of buddy-buddy Hell's Angels buzzing cherubini. Am I blissfully dying of sperm poisoning on 10 pink milligrams of a seratonin-uptake inhibitor, self-betrayed? Mom playgirled Dad. Splitsville. Elvis Nutty Buddied into oblivion. Frig it. Word.

# Steven F. White

## Under Her Window: Ouro Prêto

I imagine her building a life here
with pieces of New England,
writing on a stone past in this Brazil
that enslaves my breath, mines my steps.
Leaving and entering shadow
as they move on steep, cobbled streets,
there are children dressed as angels
for Corpus Christi. I see the empty tombs
of rebels and time's broken fingers on display.

Now I walk the high road that goes to Mariana.
It passes the Vila Mariana:
Elizabeth Bishop named her home
in Ouro Prêto after Marianne Moore,
as if by coming here she could wrest
poems from her mentor's presence.
Bishop bought a ruined dwelling,
wrecked verse from another era
collapsed on stacked, flat stones.

She rebuilt, but preserved the seteiras:
vertical slits of fear that once opened
onto a colonial world of arrows and attacks.
She had a mantel-work of x-ray art: window
into lines of leather-bound vegetable and mineral
by some anonymous Brazilian Shakespeare.

She had her imported bathtub and woodstove.
She had a shaded room invaded by a stream of spirits.
She had a garden for all her anguish.

Her view of this jewel of a city must have broken
those refractory New England dreams in Minas.
And now I am under her window
where she, the unobservable foreigner,
listened to herself and to the voices
of all those who drank the fountain's ice-cold water.
This home and its visitors are part of her geographies.
If I, too, am producing a map in progress,
I also become the places that create me.

I walk down to the city in darkness
illuminated by splendid façades.

# *Fiction*

# Roberta Allen

## Every Man's Nightmare

After listening to her obsess for an hour on my speakerphone, my ex-boyfriend called her "every man's nightmare." I don't remember exactly what she said, only her hysterical voice as she spoke about the man she'd gone out with the evening before, a man she liked who, in the moment of trying to kiss her goodnight, unleashed every demon she normally drowned in red wine, but, evidently, she hadn't had enough red wine to drink, or maybe there wasn't enough red wine in all the liquor stores combined in Ulster County to drown the fear his attempted kiss let loose, which made her tell him, probably with the same breathless rush of words I was hearing on the phone that another woman they both knew was much better suited to him than she would ever be, and that she'd be happy to give him her number since she was incapable of having an intimate relationship or, for that matter, a casual relationship with him or anyone else, so sure was she that she'd wind up ruining everything, which is exactly what she did, without even having, what could have been for someone else, the sweetness of a kiss.

# Jay Baruch

## A Little Heart

The ER doctor intubates the year-old boy. A column of vomit rises up the breathing tube. He suctions out sour smelling chunks from tiny lungs. Two ER nurses work busily. The doctor hears the younger nurse breathing fast, imagines the boy's father discovering the infant motionless in his crib, two hours after putting him to bed. The doctor has a son the same age, and wonders if he's sleeping safely through the night. His son vomits often: formula, milk, baby food of all kinds. This could be his son, the doctor thinks. He looks at the stone-faced father standing at the foot of the infant's stretcher, tugging low the brim of his Red Sox cap, embracing his quietly tearing wife from behind. The doctor and his wife could be these parents.

No, the doctor reminds himself. His wife is a meticulous mother. He's a savvy and cautious father. Besides, these parents look like kids themselves: the father lost in scruffy, oversized skateboarder clothes; the wife wearing a brown and peach fast food uniform. But it's the North Face backpack at their feet, zippered halfway, that stops the doctor's eye. Inside there are diapers, baby powder and wet wipes. The doctor is dumbfounded. On arrival, the infant's skin was a lifeless color, and the parents brought along the diaper bag. He is afraid they've watched too many doctor shows on TV and expect miracles from him. The doctor feels himself getting a little angry about this and rattles off more orders. The drugs aren't working, but he feels the pressure of the well-stocked diaper bag, much fatter than his son's diaper bag.

The younger nurse presses the heel of her hand into the infant's elastic chest. She's trembling, trying to count out a rhythm in her head. The parents are standing there, watching, which only makes her tremble more. What would they say if they knew this was her first infant code? What if this was her child and the nurse doing chest compressions was fresh out of nursing school? Now the younger nurse is really trembling. There's a dry sucking sensation at the back of her throat. She thinks she may have to vomit and eyes the nearest garbage container.

The younger nurse looks over at the older nurse. The older nurse isn't much older than the younger nurse, but she's been a nurse for fifteen years and it shows; weathered skin, bags under tender green eyes, a fit body, a smoker's cough.

The older nurse is giving medication through the IV. She stares at the clock high on the wall. She yawns. She looks expectantly and impatiently at the doctor. She shakes her head. She glances up at the clock again. "Call it," she whispers to the doctor, "You're giving them hope."

"That's all I have to give," the doctor whispers back to the older nurse.

"Shame on you," says the older nurse.

"Parents need to know we did absolutely everything."

"No," says the older nurse, trying to keep her voice down. "They need honesty. The hard truth."

The older nurse is tough and practical. Her daughter is serving time in a women's prison in upstate New York. The older nurse is now raising her two granddaughters, each from different fathers who, the older nurse believes, are in prison, too.

The older nurse hates pointless behavior. She likes the doctor, but doesn't like working with him because if there is a point to his actions, he doesn't point it out to her. The younger nurse told her once she considered the doctor thoughtful. Now the older nurse really doesn't like the younger nurse. But the older nurse knows the younger nurse is like so many other younger nurses, ripe with optimism and nervous energy. And one day, the younger nurse will become an older nurse, and when this happens, she might like her more.

*

The doctor explains to the parents how a heartbeat now would be cruel. It would pump blood to a dead brain.

"We understand," the father says. "How about five more minutes?"

The older nurse drops her head, looks sadly at the infant and thinks, "Poor, poor, child." She leans close to the doctor's ear.

"Nice going."

"Give another round of epi," the doctor says.

"But this is the last round," the older nurse whispers. "The fifteenth round. After this, the fight's over."

The doctor nods his head. "We'll see. We might have to go into extra innings.

"Extra innings! There are no extra innings in boxing."

"This isn't boxing," says the doctor, solemnly.

*

The older nurse asks the young parents if they wish to hold the infant's hand. Both the mother and father respond with opaque stares. The older nurse moves her index finger through the palm of the infant's dough-soft skin. She motions to the mother to come over. The mother's petite body freezes. Her brunette hair is cut short. Large, silver hoops jingle from her ears as she shakes her head, no. The older nurse takes the mother's hand, and with a gentle tug, places it on her child's. The mother wells up with tears. She snorts loudly, looks back over her shoulder to the father, who turns and leaves the room.

*

Nausea sits at the very back of the younger nurse's throat. She's confident nothing worse will come in its place. She's been pressing the infant's chest for over forty minutes. Concentrating so intently on the nausea distracts the younger nurse from the reality of what she's doing. A cool monotony washes over her.

Initially, the younger nurse has to fight off her own tears, the sick feeling in her belly, but now she's hungry. She's bored and hungry. The younger nurse moves a half step, gives the mother room to hold her infant's hand. But the infant is small, and the younger nurse must continue pressing his chest, so she and the mother are rubbing shoulders. The mother smells of greasy food, and this makes the younger nurse hungrier. Thinking about food distracts the younger nurse. In her entire life she can't recall ever being this hungry.

*

Cardiac resuscitation is a recipe to be followed. The doctor concentrates on the infant when he needs to. But his mind wanders. He thinks of how his son sleeps. Diapered butt thrust into the air, chubby hands pillowing cheeks wet with drool. When the doctor looks down, it's his son whose skin is mottled at the ears and back. And the young mother now looks like his wife.

He fights the urge to leave the bedside and call home. Wake his wife; wake up his son, too. Maybe roust up the dog. Make sure the whole family is breathing.

The young father returns to the room, hands deep into his pockets, his jeans pulled low on the hips. The doctor looks at him with embarrassment. The mother's eyes are squeezed shut. The doctor closes his eyes, too, takes an exhausted breath. He still sees his son in the front of his head, not with his eyes, but just as clearly. It could happen, the doctor can't help but acknowledge to himself. The unimaginable is possible.

*

The doctor calls the code; declares the time of death. 3:45 a.m. The younger nurse covers her mouth in shock, as if stumbling upon the infant for the first time. She watches the older nurse sponge the infant clean; first the head, then the arms and chest, then the pudgy legs and back. The younger nurse can't believe what the older nurse does next. She takes a diaper from the parent's bag, secures it tight around the infant and places him in the mother's arms. The mother's face becomes a knot of unexpected joy and unbearable grief. The mother holds the infant in the crook of her arm, brings his face to her chest, and slowly, cautiously begins to sway, humming low, as if lulling her son to sleep. The younger nurse starts crying. The older nurse shoots her a look that says "Stop that."

The younger nurse leaves the ER, strolls the parking lot. The night is warm, muggy, teeming with stars. The need for tears has past. She can see the father leaning back against a red pick-up, the radio playing low, cigarette aimed towards the sky. She walks to the ambulance entrance. On a far curb, in the otherwise quiet darkness, she sees the doctor sitting, face buried in his hands, shoulders heaving. The younger nurse walks over, anxiously looking for someone to share her grief. She places her hand on the doctor's shoulders. "Go inside," the doctor says through his palms

*

The doctor, the older nurse and the younger nurse sit in the break room, sipping burnt coffee. They don't say a word to each other. There are many other places to sit, but they chose the same square coffee-stained table. There are two defrosted burritos in the microwave that smells of freezer burn. "If you called the code sooner," says the older nurse, "we wouldn't have missed the roach coach."

The younger nurse is surprised by the harsh tone. She thinks it disrespectful.

The doctor looks up sleepily. "Are you saying I should make medical decisions based on when the food truck comes?" he asks.

The younger nurse turns her head from side to side, like watching a tennis match, crunching thoughtfully into raw sticks of carrots and celery.

The older nurse rips the packaging from another burrito.

"The kid looked like he'd been down forever on arrival." She takes a bite.

"You weren't thinking of the parents. You definitely weren't thinking about the roach coach."

"Hey, that's my burrito," says the doctor.

The older nurse chews ravenously. "Not anymore."

\*

The night moves in a slow, dopey haze. The younger nurse feels like all the blood has been drained out of her. She has to care for other patients now. The code is over, but thoughts of the infant shadow her. A bulky young man with a twisted ankle screams at her for waiting so long. He's in pain. She's unsure if she should tell him about the dead infant. She apologizes for the wait, informs him that they've been busy with a very sick child.

"I've been here half the night," yells the young man.

"Shh," says the older nurse, striding boldly towards the young man. "A child died tonight. We're not in the mood."

"But …"

"Behave yourself," says the older nurse. "Or I'm going to put you in time out."

The younger nurse approaches the older nurse in the medication room.

"How do you move on as if it was no big deal?"

The older nurse draws medication into a syringe. There's an air bubble. "Just … like … this," says the older nurse, flicking her finger several times against the outside of the syringe. The bubble rises to the surface and disappears.

\*

The doctor's wife is unhappy that her husband has called in the middle of the night. Now their son is crying and the dog is yelping. He explains to her why he had to call. "Listen to what's going on here now," she says to him. He hears his son shrieking, and the dog is barking madly. "You weren't thinking," she says.

"Oh no!" he says. "You don't understand."

"You weren't thinking," says the wife.

\*

Hearing his son's piercing cry clears the doctor's head; the image of the dead infant curls away from the image of his son. Over the next few hours, the doctor finds it easier to focus on other patients.

But then the young mother returns to the ER. She walks into the treatment area holding a healthy boy that looks exactly like the dead infant. A neat, gray-haired gentleman walks beside her, his steps slowing to keep pace with hers.

The doctor blinks, knuckles his eyes; it's really her moving towards him, the familiar backpack stuffed with diapers slung over one shoulder. The infant is breathing. He's sucking on a pacifier.

\*

The younger nurse crosses her chest, hugs herself, and shakily lowers into a chair. "I don't think I'm cut out for this," she says.

"None of us are," says the doctor.

"Speak for yourself," says the older nurse, standing with a fist on her hip.

The younger nurse wonders if the older nurse was a hard ass as a younger nurse. She watches the doctor button his white coat, straighten his back, and rub his chin. He appears calm and pensive, as if dead patients typically return healthy to the ER. When the younger nurse last saw the mother, she was holding the infant tight across her arms in the same exact way. Now the fear has returned. The younger nurse can't decide what's more frightening: watching a healthy infant die, or a dead infant come back to life.

*

The doctor tries not to look at the infant, but he hears slurps and yawns.

"I'm a caseworker from child protective services," says the gentleman.

The doctor is surprised to get such a strong handshake from someone wearing a worn corduroy sport jacket and crinkled slacks.

"So," says the doctor, trying to hold himself together. "What can I do for you?"

"Take a look at the boy," says the caseworker.

The doctor hears the younger nurse gasp behind him.

"OK," the doctor says. "Then what?"

"The infant who died a few hours ago, this is his twin brother."

"Twin?" the doctor says.

"I need this one examined for evidence of abuse."

\*

The older nurse looks at the mother; head slung low, wet hair touching the shoulders of her white T-shirt, which hangs to the ripped knees of her jeans. She's alone. The father isn't with her. This could be her daughter, the older nurse thinks.

"Abuse? How can you be so cruel?" the doctor asks, loudly.

The older nurse listens in when the caseworker pulls the doctor aside.

"The boyfriend left the children alone. He put the kids to bed, then ran across the street to hang out with his buddies at the liquor store."

"That guy was the boyfriend?" the doctor asks. "Where was mom?"

"Mom was at work."

The older nurse catches the mother wiping tears with the back of her wrist. She admires the mother's steely toughness. Their eyes lock. Neither one blinks.

\*

"Boyfriend?" the doctor thinks to himself, lifting the sleeping boy into his arms. The boy groggily reaches for the mother. She rubs the boy's back, whispers that it's OK. The boy resists lowering to the stretcher. The doctor wants to hold the infant, not examine him. He knows he can't think that way. With the mother's help, the doctor undresses the infant. There's dirt beneath toenails and fingernails, in the creases of feet and hands. There are black-and-blue marks on his knees, the size of quarters, and scratches on both elbows. The doctor's son is marked with similar toddler wounds.

"What do you think?" the caseworker asks the doctor later in the privacy of the medication room.

"I'm comfortable sending him home."

The caseworker exhales. His breath smells of mint and nicotine. "We have an active file on them," the caseworker says.

"Sure, there's bruising, but that doesn't mean abuse," the doctor says.

"We're taking custody of the child until we can investigate further."

"Is that really necessary?" the doctor asks. "My kid has bruises everywhere. He falls down and gets banged up."

"That's your kid," says the caseworker. He scratches his neck, shakes his head while skimming papers in a manila folder. "I have no choice," says the caseworker, as he opens the door to leave the medication room and inform the mother.

"No. You can't," the mother wails. "Please don't."

The mother's eyes dart from the doctor to the younger nurse. "Please," she says, her voice cracking.

The older nurse looks down at her clogs, clicking against the floor.

The younger nurse raises her voice. She stops when the older nurse tugs the back of her shoulder and whispers in her ear, "Careful, you're crossing the line."

The younger nurse slips a box of tissues within arm's reach of the mother, rolls her eyes and bristles at the older nurse, then walks away.

"Do something," the mother begs the doctor. The doctor opens his mouth but catches himself. What can he say? Twice in one night he couldn't return her child to her.

# Charles Blackstone

## 37%

"I need to talk to you."

"Why?"

"Zach and I sort of broke up."

"Sort of? How sort of?"

"I don't know.... I guess it had been coming for a long time, you know the story with him, and the porn, and the ... I don't know, the ambivalence ... and so, yeah, that's it."

"So what are you going to do now? Are you going to move out?"

"We're stuck in this lease."

"How much longer do you have?"

"A year."

"How do you have a year?"

"I don't know ... don't make this hard for me. Okay?"

"Just tell me why it is you have a year left on your lease. How is that even possible?"

"We resigned recently. That's how."

"How recently?"

"A week or two ago. I don't remember. I haven't been myself lately. God. You really know how to turn everything around, don't you."

"I'm not turning anything around. I'm just trying to understand."

"So understand. Do you understand? It's over. Over."

"Okay, fine, it's over. So are you going to leave DC?"

"I can't leave. I'm stuck in this lease."

"What is he going to do? Make you stay? Can he do that?"

"I don't think he can do that. I mean, he shouldn't be able to do that. I just want to do what's fair."

"You're probably the only person I know who thinks about how to break up with someone fairly. Most people just grab what they can take and run."

"Yeah, well, you know that's not me. I mean, you should know that's not how I am. I may be stubborn at times, maybe a little mean—"

"Ruthless, I'd say."

"Okay, ruthless. But I'm principled. Always principled."

"Whose name is the place in?"

"Both of ours. Well, his. His, really. I'm not on the lease."

"So you can go, then. Right?"

"No, not right. I can't really go."

"Why not?"

"I'm kind of like-god, this is embarrassing."

"Just tell me. This is getting frustrating."

"I'm sort of the co-signer. I don't even know what the hell we set up. My name isn't on the place, but if Zach stops paying, well, I'm fucked."

"Can he afford to keep living there on his own?"

"No ... I mean, at least I don't think he can."

"Will he find a roommate?"

"He said he won't live with anyone."

"So where does that leave you?"

"Exactly what I said!"

"Seriously, though. Where does that leave you?"

"Fucked, I guess."

"What does he expect you're going to do? He can't seriously think that you're going to pay half the rent—"

"Sixty-three percent."

"Sixty-three percent?"

"Yeah, that's what I pay."

"How do you figure?"

"Uh, do you want me to get a calculator? You can check my work. The rent's two thousand and I—"

"Two thousand dollars for a one-bedroom? Jesus."

"Don't get me started. It's a junior one-bedroom, too."

"So how do you figure this sixty-three percent?"

"Well, I don't know how we ended up at this figure-well, maybe I do, but whatever, he pays … Okay, I pay twelve-sixty and he pays the rest. Seven forty. That's his share. The worst part is that he's been using the parking space."

"You don't have a car."

"No, no, I don't. You're right."

"Why does he only pay— "

"Thirty-seven percent?"

"Yeah. Why is Zach only responsible for thirty-seven percent of your rent? The rent for the apartment which you and he both share equally, as in fifty-fifty?"

"Shared. Remember this is all past tense now."

"Shared. Fine. Why?"

"That's what he was paying when he was renting the attic apartment from his parents and, well, I liked this place. He said it was too much. Not like he couldn't afford it. He just didn't want to pay it. He said he couldn't think of himself living in a two-thousand dollar apartment. But, as I said, I liked it, and I didn't really care what he thought."

"But he was kind of an important factor in the decision-making process, wouldn't you say?"

"I wouldn't say an important factor. Or maybe just not all-important."

"No, no. Certainly not."

"Anyway, so, yeah, I wanted the place, he didn't want to pay more than he was paying, and, so …we did it."

"Do you still think it was worth it?"

"Well, it was worth it until he started becoming more interested in his stack of porn magazines. It was worth it until staying up until two in the morning, with one hand on an Xbox controller and the other on a crust of Pizza Hut Supreme hand-tossed was the only thing he wanted to do, preferably without me in the room, probably so he could put his hand down his pants in between slices."

"It was until you had to pay sixty-three percent of an apartment you're not living in."

"I don't want to pay for it. It's so unfair."

"I don't think you should have to either."

"He's going to force me to."

"Just say no."

"I can't. I'm not strong enough."

"Well don't look at me. I can't give you advice. I say yes way more often than I say no."

"You're the strongest person I know."

"If I'm the strongest person you know, you know a lot of weak people. I had several post-dinner spoons of peanut butter on two occasions last week. One time I was a little tipsy. It's a large container, so I think I took more liberties with it than I would have had it been a small container."

"Still. Can I move in with you?"

"Yeah, right."

"No, seriously. Can I?"

"We live in two separate cities, for one thing. For another, I happen to be engaged to marry someone … I can't believe I just listed those things in that order. Obviously my being engaged trumps matters of geography."

"Come on, Sam. Live with me. Let me live with you."

"I can't. What about Wendy? What would she think?"

"She won't even notice me around. Come on. This is a victimless crime."

"Not if Zach finds out you and your sixty-three percent have taken up residence in Chicago."

"Don't think about that. Just say yes."

"Can we just settle for me telling you that you're crazy and offering to help you surf Craigslist for a few hours tomorrow afternoon?"

"God, I should have known you'd do this to me."

"Do what to you? And when did you decide that you wanted to live with me?"

"You make me sound all premeditated. I didn't plan this out."

"It seems like you at least gave it some thought."

"It just occurred to me now, during this very conversation, that it might be … I don't know … somewhat logical to stay with you. At least for a little while."

"And the being engaged to someone else part. That didn't enter into your reasoning."

"No, it didn't. But I don't see why that would be such an impossible obstacle. I mean, we broke up years ago. And we were hardly together at all."

"The best worst three weeks of my life."

"So what's the big deal? We've been friends for a while now. I see you when I come into town. We have coffee, just like this. I go back to DC and we email and talk on the phone once in a while when you're drunk at some bar where neither of us can hear anything. So now we'll do the same things. Except for—"

"Except for the fact that you'll be living in my guest room."

"Yeah, right! I forgot about that part! You even have a room with a door. Here I was thinking about your old place and getting myself all ready for couch life with a clothesline of thongs festooned between the windows and the TV."

"Don't get too excited. It's the same couch that you remember from two years ago. But, yeah, it's in a room. And the room has a door."

"Even better!"

"Though I'm extremely amused by this premise, and think there are loads of sitcom-worthy possibilities here: ex-girlfriend moves into apartment with ex-boyfriend and his current fiancée, I can't really escape the main issue."

"What's the main issue?"

"Wendy. You remember her, right? The headstrong young magazine editor who rounds out our ensemble cast? She hasn't said yes yet. Actually she hasn't even heard about this yet.... Unless you've told her."

"No, I haven't told her. Why would I have told her? She and I don't talk. We've never even met."

"We'll have to correct that. If we're going to get anywhere with your plan."

"My plan? Have I not won at least your preliminary approval?"

"I haven't decided yet."

"Okay. Well, let me know when you make up your mind."

"Trust me. You'll be the first to know."

# Lee Byrd

## Lazy Heart of Mine

I am cranky because Ofe and her shadow Titi—who had quit coming to see me for over a year—came visiting at 6 a.m. one morning last week, when Bill and I were still lying sound asleep, our feet hanging out the end of the bed. Believe it or not, I'd often imagined the two of them walking freely and sin vergüenza into our bedroom like that—one of the doors to our bedroom opens outside to a little patio, which you can get to just by walking in the side gate—and standing at the bottom of our bed like a vision, holding hands.

I am curious why I am surrounded by these particular people. Why didn't I get the everyday companions other people seem to have?

In a book of mediations I read every morning, the author says, "Watch the kind of people God brings around you, and you will be humiliated to find that this is His way of revealing to you the kind of person you have been to Him."

### Ofe et al

I was looking out the door this morning, just around ten. Just a peek. Just a hair so the neighbors don't think I'm spying. I see Ofe bracing herself against the edge of her porch's stoop with her hand, her daughter Titi holding onto her other hand. Ofe's a short old woman—I'm 78, Annie!—made shorter—and shrinking—by bad feet, long toenails, knees that buckle, and legs that bow. Maybe a giant in her day, who knows?—we didn't know her then. She's been our neighbor for 25 years—Ofelia Negrete. And she is coming to visit.

My husband and I talk. Do we have it in ourselves to offer her coffee, maybe breakfast? After all, she is heading our way. Many minutes later—the minutes it takes her to walk down her driveway, along the sidewalk past Nora's house next door, and up my front steps—I look out the front door and there she and Titi are, no surprise, holding hands, perched on my porch step, ready to come in. There is no stopping Ofe once she comes down off her porch. Even if you were to yell out, I'm busy, or run ahead to meet her and tell her—in the style people used in New Jersey where I grew up—that you weren't receiving visitors right then, or stop her at the front door and say you were just about to go out to the store, she would say, No, no, I know you busy, Annie, I just gonna sit down here on your front porch. What I gonna do at home? And she would sit, whether you were there or not, as if her lack of things to do were your responsibility. You would feel terribly guilty for having made excuses with her sitting there on your front porch.

And, of course, it is no good whatsoever to implore Titi—who you might assume to be the more responsible party—she's 39 years old—to have some understanding of your situation—I want the morning to myself!—and reverse directions. Her understanding is—to say the least—extraordinary, oblivious to the niceties of protecting your Saturday order. No. It is much better to get yourself completely prepared the minute you see Ofe and Titi coming.

Ofe's been ready to visit since last night because many things, according to her, happened in the nighttime, things to last a lifetime, just between the time we went to bed and the time we woke up. Gilbert, her son who lives at home, now just 27, had a heat stroke, though—as my husband pointed out— there is no heat at night. It is close to fall: the cooler weather has already arrived. But no matter. It was a heat stroke as Ofe reported it. Rudy, another son, came over in the night when the news broke and he took Gilbert to the county hospital, and they said that Gilbert—no news to any of us—needed to stop drinking and start eating. Otherwise, heat strokes would be common. But Gilbert, Ofe's son, says that he wants to go to be with his father, Nacho Senior, who is now dead. His way of getting there is to drink from the minute he rolls out of bed and to continue on through the day and into the dark night, with only a brief hard nap or two in between to sustain him and no food—absolutely no food: an impeccable plan.

In addition to Gilbert's heat stroke, Ofe reports, Cesar Fonseca went to jail, same reason as Gilbert going to the county hospital, a sort of neighborhood heat stroke in common. Someone in Ofe's family appealed to a female member of the Fonseca family, possibly Cesar's soon-to-be-separated-wife, to see if she wanted a ride to the jail to get Cesar out, but—Ofe reports—the soon-to-be-late wife doesn't care about Cesar. Let him rot there, she said. Also Mickey Diamanti, another Fonseca primo who had also had a heat stroke, is going to lose his legs. They smell. Been scratching and scratching them. He won't go to the doctor or take care of himself.

We look out the front window in the dining room, where now all four of us sit around our old table at breakfast: Ofe, Titi, Bill, and me. Everything is quiet, calm. It doesn't seem like anything at all could have happened in the night. We went to bed late, too, around midnight, and everything then was like it is now: perfectly quiet. So somewhere between midnight and the dawning of this new and remarkable day, the neighborhood cracked open and spilled out. Or so Ofe says.

Ofe has fixed Titi's pancakes and then her own while she talks—a production worthy of Andy Warhol with its painstaking detail. First Titi's pancakes and then her own must be separated and spread out flat all over the plate. Each one needs a smear of butter and then lots of syrup. They must be cut in tiny pieces, but that takes a long time and they dry out a little in the process, so once that is done, they must be syruped again. Then three heaping teaspoons of sugar in her coffee, a few obscure instructions barked at Titi, and a big smile up at me and Bill who are watching—staring! agog!—in true writerly fascination and—soup's on!

Just exactly who is Titi?

Titi is the third child of (the late) Nacho and (the current) Ofe Negrete and she is—from some points of view—retarded, though she has been given many talents and abilities to compensate.

One is the ability to smell out a party. She also speaks both Spanish and English—though it's hard to make out what she's saying in either language. She can do a number of things that most regular folks would find impossible—she can come to your house and park herself in one place for a long time, watching you and smiling and unsmiling in a regular rhythmic pattern, especially if you are talking to her mother Ofe. She can come to your house and sit in a chair all day and look at a book, and—though she can't read it or make sense of the pictures—she will be perfectly content. She—39 or thereabouts—can come to your house and squeeze up in a chair with your granddaughter Naomi who is midway between 2 and 3 years old and pass the morning away without a care. She can run with little tiny steps and giggle at the same time. If she has something on her mind—her birthday—an intense consuming preoccupation for her—or if she is excited or worried about something—Ofe has a cold or the police came to somebody's house the night before—she can come to your door and knock a dozen times a day to let you know about it. She can arrive at your doorstep or your bedroom door as early as 6 a.m.—like she did last week—or as late as ... one night, truth to tell, Titi and Ofe came over at 3 in the pitch-dark morning because they felt the need—right then—to visit.

### Someone is Peeing on My Couch

It is hard to know for certain what's going on in Ofe's house because the information about it comes from Ofe herself—or from Titi, worse—and Ofe and Titi don't recognize the minute-by-minute structure of the reigning universe. Instead, they float in time—two orphans floating on a leafy boat in the great wide river of time. The only thing they cling to is each other's hand. They rest in Time. It has no names or divisions. It is just there. Maybe it is Wednesday, maybe not, they don't know. Maybe it is 1960, maybe it is yesterday or tomorrow. Ohhh. Who knows? Maybe Ofe just had her first daughter Olga—the one she had before she met (the late) Nacho Senior—or maybe Olga's daughter Vicky is having Ofe's great-grandchild what's-her-name or what's-his-name. Maybe Titi is 9 or maybe she is 39. I don't know, she giggles. Who cares? 9:15 or 12:15 or I'll pick you up in a half hour? Just honk, Annie, I only just got to put on my dress. The only thing that matters is the egg and chorizo burrito they just ate. Mmm. It was good.

News from Ofe about this morning, then, could be stale—at least a year old—or it could be only the stuff of her imagination or her hopes or the paranoid fears brought on by her occasional breakdowns, as her family calls them—or it could be as real as the man next door falling down his steps drunk, which he is doing right now.

Today I'm on Ofe's porch and I, of course, came here really truly believing that I was only going to talk to her about sweeping her sidewalk: it is a mess, all dirt and rocks and old paper and beer cans—evidence of some dreadful activity the night before—swirling winds, drinking men, dark and unaccountable things. The whole street, in fact, is just rock and rubble and silty dirt and, in my righteous imagination, I am going up and down sweeping it clean, but Ofe wants to tell me things. Though not at first. She doesn't start out telling me things, only just passing pleasantries, like how am I and how's Bill and how's Elise and how's Arnie and how's Roy?

Then the floodgates open. Do I know who spent the night on her couch? One-armed Piano's girlfriend, the one who is pregnant with Piano's child, the one whose two little girls—not Piano's—wander up and down the street like orphans. Suddenly the girlfriend is the neighborhood's excess baggage, just the kind of baggage I will soon be at the currently-being-reengineered-gas company where I work. It seems obvious to all of us who keep our eye on the street that Piano doesn't want this girl any more. The two little girls came to Ofe's too, and spent the night with their mother. And did I know what the one did? She peed all over Ofe's couch.

Ofe's eyes get big. What you think of that, Annie? she whispers and winks her left eye very slowly at me. That's not right.

And then comes Mickey Diamanti and he spends the night too, just like it's a flop house or something. That's not right either. And she says that her other sons Nacho Junior and Rudy and Johnny and her daughters Olga and Josie and Ricky are mad at her son Gilbert because he has for his girlfriend the big fat Consuela.

## Consuela!

Consuela comes there this morning, after that long night Ofe had and Ofe not getting much sleep, and Consuela wants her car fixed and then she starts to fight with Gilbert and Ofe tells Gilbert to just leave Consuela alone, to not fix her car, just to get away from her. But Gilbert and Consuela go into his bedroom instead and close the door and they tell Ofe and Titi to go out on the porch, go out walking, go down and see Annie! Get out! Go see Mr. Fonseca. But Ofe, she doesn't want to go down to Mr. Fonseca's house because he has two bathrooms and there is one that is near his bedroom and when she was in that bathroom one day, he was peeking in at her through his window while she was peeing. And he told her once when she was down there, What about now that your husband Nacho's dead? Who do you sleep with? And she says, I sleep with Titi. And he says, What about one night if I could come down and come in your window and sleep with you?

What you think of that, Annie? Ofe's eyes get big and she shakes her head back and forth very slowly. That's not right.

## Ofe Might Move

Gilbert, Ofe's son, is back in the hospital with another heat stroke. Ofe is sitting on her fold-up metal chair in the corner of her front porch and crying. Nacho Junior, her oldest son, has declared that he is going to sell the house and give the money to Ofe and Titi and they are going to take it and move away from Gilbert and his reckless and hard-drinking friends to Brownsville to live with Ofe's sister. The question remains: What right-minded right-thinking person will buy her house, that house that smells of peed-on old couches, that is falling apart, that Sabbath the horrible devil dog has crapped all over the yard of, that years and years and years of men and boys drinking with abandon have made to crumble into ruin?

I didn't go to church again. I went down after a while to see Ofe and ask her if she wanted to take a walk. She says yes and takes Titi's hand, fastening herself up with Titi in this fashion: they grab hands, then Ofe holds Titi's hand up and puts each finger of Titi's between a finger of her own so they are neatly and perfectly laced together. On the other side of Ofe, she and I hold hands, but she doesn't care if I am laced up like Titi, she only just grabs on tight and pulls hard, she being so much shorter than me. And she is very strong. It makes my hand hurt bad. She is crushing my wedding ring against my fingers.

As we walk along, Ofe reports that Gilbert is waking her up in the night, knocking on her door— Mama! Mama! she cries out in imitation of her son—and says his dead father Nacho Senior is calling to him saying, Come with me, Gilbert, come with me. I want you to come with me. One a these times, he going to kill himself, says Ofe, peering up at me. What I gonna do, Annie?

## Mission Unaccomplished

I have before me at this desk where I write a bulletin board filled with photos I have taken. Many of them are of Ofe. She is my muse. She is a good one to get to sit for you because she does just that—sits. And never moves. And never smiles—sin sonrisa— unless you tell her a story or a joke that has a little edge or shade of meaning in it that puts another person in a difficult light— which I never do! I can take ten pictures of Ofe in the same amount of minutes and she will not have shifted a muscle unless I ask her to.

I have been taking pictures of her during the last year since Nacho Senior died. If I had had the courage, I would have taken pictures of her at Nacho's funeral—a perfectly gray overcast day, drizzling, tiny shrunken Ofe in black under an enormous black umbrella, her daughters surrounding her with their long black hair, her sons in black shirts and leather jackets, their black eyes like saucers under more black umbrellas—and me with black and white film in the camera! But no one in their right mind takes pictures at a funeral.

In all the pictures I have taken otherwise, she is pensive. She doesn't have Nacho Senior anymore to help her ignore Gilbert's drinking or to pretend not to notice the way Gilbert and Rudy and Johnny sometimes sell drugs—all those fancy cars pulling up in front of their run-down house!—or to sit inside while all of Gilbert's many friends curse the night away on her front porch—those guys need a thesaurus!

No, now that Nacho Senior is dead, Ofe has to ignore those activities all by herself, and it must be hard work, it must be taking its toll, because Ofe has lost her zip. She's shrinking even more, too. And now instead of getting dressed, she just wears housedresses. My Elise says she came to our house yesterday and showed her the sort of things you can easily show people when you're only wearing a house dress: first her knee brace, then some other scar further up her leg, and finally the thin line on her stomach that marks a C-section.

She's at the height of her visiting powers, Ofe is, and she always comes bearing the most dreadful news. Men are sleeping all over her house, peeing on her couches, fighting until all hours of the nights. One of them has even tried to crawl into bed with Titi. All her living room windows are busted out from people—mostly men, though there are occasional women—falling and crashing through them, and the swamp cooler doesn't work, the part they need would make significant inroads on Gilbert's beer money, so she sits on her front porch almost all day to catch a little bit of cool air. She has a fly swatter poised in her hand—a foolish job—in the dense summer heat. What I gonna do, Annie? she asks me. And as always—lucky people they are who live near me—I have the solution.

In my mind, all her problems stem from the fact that Gilbert drinks. If he would stop drinking, everything would change: he'd chase his friends away—no one to drink or pee or flop in the house anymore—he'd fix the windows, he'd fix the house, Ofe would be happy. But—another daydreamy leap—he's not going to quit drinking until he sees that he's an alcoholic and he's not going to see that he's an alcoholic until Ofe tells him he is and Ofe's not going to tell him he's an alcoholic until she sees it first and she's not going to see that he's an alcoholic until I show her. Me! I'm the one who's going to show her! Hallelujah!

So. The first step is to drag her to that place of understanding and then everything will tumble into place. Meanwhile, I have done some masterful supplemental research. I happened to be out walking on Piedras and I passed by this door and on it was written the West Texas Council on Alcoholism. It seemed like a sign—of the portent variety—to me. It was so close—we could walk!—and everything and all roads—at least for Ofe and her son Gilbert—seemed to lead to it. We'd walk in the door, he'd be cured, we'd walk back out the door into the bright light of sobriety.

So one Thursday I made an appointment with a counselor at the West Texas Council on Alcoholism and I took Ofe there—and, of course, Titi too because you can't take Ofe anywhere without taking Titi.

Here is what I told Ofe: I told her we were going to go and sit down and talk to someone about her Gilbert and his drinking, but she didn't really seem to understand at all what my intentions were. Or maybe she did, and she just thought she'd go to be polite, or to humor me, or to give me just enough rope to hang myself, which is about how everyone in the neighborhood is with me.

Anyway, I was late getting off from my job at the gas company. Our appointment was for 2:30 and I didn't even leave downtown until 2:15 and then there was the train blocking Piedras and people and cars in the way, all sorts of obstructions—as if God was telling me to stay out of Ofe's business—and then I had to go get her at her house and she and Titi weren't ready, are never ready, have no conception of late—or early—for that matter.

When we finally arrived, the counselor said that he couldn't meet with us—his supervisor had told him that he had another emergency appointment.

How could that be? I asked. We are an emergency! And we had an appointment even if we are late! Can't you see—I pointed in Ofe and Titi's direction—what sort of an emergency we are? This woman's son is drinking himself to death, we don't have a lot of time to waste here. Then I got mad. I said I wanted to talk to his supervisor. And I yelled at that poor man and harangued him in as irritating a New Jersey style as I could muster. Finally, the supervisor said he would cancel another appointment and he would see us himself. By then it was nearly 4 o'clock. I was terribly upset, while Ofe and Titi—oblivious to time and insistings—had hardly moved a muscle except for that ongoing grinning and ungrinning that Titi does with her face.

The supervisor took us to his tiny room—a room with a door and walls but no ceiling, just space enough for him and his big desk facing Ofe and Titi and me sitting on brought-in metal fold-up chairs.

The supervisor was in his mid-forties, with dark protruding eyes. He reminded me of those leering villainous people that Brueghel painted leaning against Christ while He sat at the supper table—though they fawned over Him, their every pop-eyed glance showed that they were as willing as anybody to see Him dead.

But this man before us was kind. He himself, as he said during the course of our interview, had had a nervous breakdown and was a former alcoholic.

He began the interview by asking Ofe what the problem was. She didn't head directly for the issue, particularly since she didn't quite know what the issue was. After all, this was my deal more than hers.

First she gave a little talk about her dead husband Nacho Senior—how she met him down on Durazno Street at a funeral, how he said Hello, how you doing and she said, Hello, how you doing, back, how he said he didn't mind that she had already had a child, he would marry her....

That speech lasted close to five minutes.

Then she talked about Titi—how Titi hangs the wash every day and how she sweeps the floor in the dining room and in the living room and in her bedroom and in the kitchen and in the basement and on the porch.... Another five minutes, during which she kept tapping Titi on the chest and Titi smiled and unsmiled and wrinkled her face up so you could see her teeth.

Finally the counselor said to Ofe, Vamanos, would you? Let's go, let's get to your son Gilbert. So then Ofe told the supervisor her Gilbert was a good boy and that he cooks chorizo and eggs in the morning and for lunch he makes the sopa and that Gilbert's friends come over to her house all the time. She leaned forward and knocked on the desk three times in imitation of the way they knock on her front door. The friends say, Hello, Mrs. Negrete. Then she says, Hello, how you doing?

Vamanos, said the counselor again.

Then she told the supervisor that Gilbert's friends call him on the phone all the time. They say, Hello, Mrs. Negrete, and then she says, Hello, how you doing? Who you want to talk to? She has to tell them that Gilbert can't talk on the phone because he's in the rest room.

Vamanos!

Then they say, Ofe continued unconcerned, Okay, Mrs. Negrete, I call him back in ten minutes....

Is there a problem in your house? said the counselor finally.

She looked at him and squinched up her face and gave a big smile and a little laugh. Oh no, she said.

Your son doesn't drink?

Only beer, she said, putting her hands up flat in front of her. See? Empty! No problems!

They were talking in Spanish, so I missed all the innuendoes and most of the point, but I think he was saying, or maybe yelling that Ofe reminded him of his own grandmother, who was always protecting him and always saying that he never did anything wrong, even though he was always always always doing something very wrong. You've got to realize, he told her, that your son is an alcoholic and there's not a thing we can do until he figures that out and until you do, too.

No, she said, he not an al-co-haul-i-co. He's a good boy.

And with that sentence the interview ended—as did—though only temporarily—my campaign to straighten Ofe's life out.

### Same Old, Same Old

My husband Bill and I went to Austin to live for six months and then we came back, but nothing seemed to have changed, at least with Ofe. As soon as we pulled up at the curb in front of our house, Ofe and Titi came down to visit. Ofe reported that Nacho Junior had come that morning early. He was knock, knock, knocking on her door—here she knocked on my window sill to prove that fact—and he was telling his little son Nacho the Third to hide down low so Grandma couldn't see and then Nacho Junior came in the house and was giving orders to Gilbert—his brother—saying this can't happen anymore, no more drinking in the house and he was telling Mickey Diamanti to get out—get off the couch!—and he was telling Ofe that he was going to send her and Titi for a visit to Brownsville.

But, of course, it was Nacho Junior himself who said nearly a year and two months ago that he would fix the 17 busted-out windows in Ofe's house and now this long later they are still busted out and it is very likely, very possible, that Ofe only dreamed this early morning visit of Nacho's. But it was such good news about Nacho's triumphant straightening out of the house, I wanted to believe it—and I'd been away so long—and then—like the icing on the cake—Ofe declared that her Gilbert is an alcoholic. The doctor has said so. At last she understands!

She also said that a man and his wife and their two kids had moved in to live with her for three months while we were gone. I was instantly very curious about this. I wondered what sort of people would want to move in with Ofe.

I asked her where they were and she said they were not there any more, and that she didn't like the woman because she was very very fat—as fat as Gilbert's Consuelo—and always bossing her around and she didn't like the man because he was drinking drinking drinking and Nacho Junior had come and thrown them all out.

Where did they come from? How do you know them? Ofe's hands went up flat in front of her—she shrugged her shoulders and puckered up her mouth. I don't know, Annie, somebody told them to come to my house, but I don know who it is. But they're not there no more.

She also reported, as usual, that there were men drinking and peeing all over the house.

But, later, when I talked about this to Nacho Junior, he said that it was Ofe herself who was leaking leaking leaking on the couches and her children had told her she better wear some diapers, but she said no, she didn't need no diapers.

Then the next day early—our first real day back from Austin—I am out on my front porch and I hear men's voices somewhere, but where I'm not sure. So I go stand out on my sidewalk and look over across the Fritze's yard to Ofe's house. It sounds like Ofe's son Gilbert with some of his friends but I can't see him or them, so I am craning my neck and peering over and suddenly a somewhat shortish man jumps into my vision, leaping from behind Alberto Fritze's house, a man who looks impish and clever like a monkey. He smiles and waves, and he has curly hair and from where I stand he looks a little like Mickey Diamanti, so I think it is Mickey, and I wave back, but I realize it's not Mickey.

Later I find out from my daughter Elise that it is the man of that couple who had lived in Ofe's house. Now that he has been thrown out of Ofe's house, it has been reported that he sneaks back to drink with Gilbert Negrete late in the night and that he has set up an office of sorts at the phone booth in the parking lot of the Quality Super Market on the corner of Wheeling and Alabama, standing in that very spot all day and taking and making phone calls—conducting business in the open air!

I go back up on my porch so I won't be staring so shamelessly and I peer over at the Negrete's house again, this time under the cover of the various potted plants on my porch. Titi is out in the early light standing in the middle of her side yard, still sleepy, her hair uncombed and sticking up—a new day, and she to her task. She heads toward the back of her house. Going to hang out the ropa? No. I hear the sound of beer bottles clanking. Did those men, those men who drink with Gilbert all day and all night—one of whom just popped into my vision—just get up from their place on the curb in the driveway between the Fritze's and the Negrete's? Did they just finish their beer drinking at seven in the morning? Or did they just start? Did Ofe send Titi out to clean up the beer bottles?

Nobody should have to live like this, I conclude, especially not an old woman like Ofe—sitting on her porch without a thing to do all day—all those drunks congregating around her, cursing and fighting—no one at all taking care of her.

Clearly I'll have to resume keeping my eagle-eye on her. Good thing I'm back in town. It would be perfect if all those drunks would sober up, or—barring that—get thrown in jail. This life must be really getting Ofe down, making her terribly depressed, so what she needs is ... something to do ... some entertainment...

I've got it! She could spend the day at one of those senior citizen centers, dancing with guys her age and playing bingo and making crocheted dolls to cover the rolls of toilet paper that Titi comes down twice a week to borrow from us. Doing a little chair aerobics, eating a free lunch, meeting and making new friends. And, of course, Titi—though she is somewhere in the vicinity of 39 and clearly not a senior citizen—could go with her. Everyone would understand—senior citizens are very kind.

So I make a few phone calls and it turns out the closest and the newest senior citizen center is up Piedras about two miles in Grandview Park—the Sacramento Senior Citizen's Center. And I call ahead and ask if Ofe can come and what's required and then I explain a little bit about Titi and how Titi is a little slow, retarded actually, and how Ofe and Titi can't be separated and how Titi is about 39 years old though she thinks she's nine or ten and then I ask if Titi can come and this guy—with the usual density of guys—says he thinks it's okay, bring Ofe up and see if she likes it.

So I go over and sit on Ofe's front porch with her and explain about this place and how it will give her something to do all day instead of sitting in the very spot where she is now glued and ask her does she want to go and she says yes. What I gonna do here all day? she asks me, as if she's been waiting for me to take her to the senior citizens' center forever.

Ofe and Titi agree to come over the next morning so I can drive them up to take a look. If you like it, I tell Ofe as we drive along, you can spend the day there and just call me when you need a ride home. If you don't like it, you can come home with me.

No, Annie, I gonna like it, Ofe declares.

This man who runs the Sacramento Center is in his mid-40s and is new at the job. He doesn't yet—and from all appearances, will never—have the senior ladies under control. They run things, always have and always will! He takes us around for a little tour. We go to a very brightly lit room where a bunch of ladies are sitting around painting ceramics—Virgin Marys and little Dutch girls carrying flower baskets and sugar jars and creamers. This is really where Ofe wants to be, putting a blue wash on some ashtray in the shape of Texas, but the man persuades her to come look at the rest of the place first. There are rooms where you can sit and visit and there is a big lunchroom with here and there some women talking, arms folded up over their chests, and in this room ensues a discussion with the supervisor about lunch.

Lunch, he says, is free to people who have been approved but you have to get on a waiting list to get approved and the waiting list—as with all government things—only opens up every October and October is two months away and otherwise lunch is $3.25 a day. Or you can bring your own. Ohhhhh, Ofe says, looking at me.

You and Titi can bring your lunch, I tell her. And we'll get you on the waiting list.

And then the guy shows us where the bingo room is and then another room where someone from the community college is talking about something or another—taxes, maybe, or social security, or making a will—but there's only one old lady in attendance, probably the only one in the Sacramento Senior Citizen's Center who has any disposable income.

What do you want to do? I ask Ofe when the tour's over.

I wanna stay here, she tells me.

Where do you want to go then?

I wanna paint the dolls.

So I take her back to the room where the ladies are all sitting around the very big table and painting ceramics. A lady at the end of the table says, Come in, come in, pasale, señora, and Ofe and Titi come in and sit down as if they'd been coming to the Sacramento Senior Citizen's Center all their lives.

I remind Ofe to call me when she is ready to come home. I have already written my phone number down on a piece of paper which she has crumpled up in her purse and I have given the same phone number to the man who runs the place.

Well, sounds like a good plan, no?

And it would have been a good plan—a great plan—if Ofe wasn't Ofe and if Titi wasn't Titi and if Titi was clearly a senior citizen and if the women at the center —bossy classless class-conscious types, reckoning that Ofe was a cut beneath them— had realized somewhere in their old pitiless hearts that Titi and Ofe can't be separated any more than a hand can be cut off from its body. It would have been a good plan if Ofe had brought money for lunch or if Ofe had brought a whole and satisfying lunch from home and it would have been a really great plan if Ofe hadn't cheated at bingo.

Although there were a number of other things that contributed to Ofe's leaving the Sacramento Senior Citizen Center after just a month or so. Assuredly, her not getting a free lunch was a big factor. The business about the waiting list and getting on the waiting list in October was not a thing to be understood or remembered or taken into consideration—just one more thing in the list of things she chose to freely ignore. Every day there was a something she did to provoke the incumbent senior citizens, who carefully guarded their rights to government food, to look down on her in regard to that precious free lunch. If she brought her own lunch—always not quite enough, a couple of burritos packed up in a lunch box that belonged to her grandson—she would try to take some iced tea and cookies from the food line. If anyone called her on that—and the women always did—she would claim that she intended to pay, though all she ever brought in her crumpled up cloth purse was a few pennies for bingo. I pay tomorrow, she'd tell whoever her accuser was. After all, everyone else was getting a free lunch. Why not her? Were they better than her or something? Why did she have to wait on some list when everyone else was eating like there was no tomorrow? But all these remarks she kept to herself.

Or if she didn't bring her lunch, she sat in the lunch room with Titi anyway, the two of them as motionless as the desert air in summer, until the supervisor or one of the cooks finally relented and gave them a plate. And then there was hell to pay among the gossiping old women that afternoon.

Another thing that Ofe cited as a reason for leaving the center was her inability to get a ride home. Now, the city had a special bus that could have picked Titi and Ofe up in the morning and brought them home in the afternoon. But once they signed up for the bus, they would have had to stick to a schedule. They couldn't have continued in the time-less pattern Ofe had always had in all her doings. Some days she decided to go to the center at 8 am and other days to stay home and sleep in bed and other days to go at 11 and then to leave whenever she felt like it or when one of the ladies said a cross word to her.

So the bus and its relentless timetable was not an option—at least not until Ofe stopped being Ofe.

Instead, I would take her when she came over to my house in the mornings and pick her up when she called for a ride home in the afternoons. Her son Gilbert couldn't take her because he didn't have a car, and his friends, who did have cars, couldn't take her because they only came to his house to drink and not to carry his mother anywhere and her son-in-law, Josie's husband, Big Beto, who lived close enough by, couldn't take her because even though he did have a car and didn't have a job, he was busy busy busy with other bodily transferences he had to perform (his wife to work, his kids to different schools and/or to baseball practice and part-time jobs) and Ofe's trip to the senior citizen center didn't count for much.

But, Ofe said, she could never get me on the telephone, even though—since I got laid off at the gas company—I was always there. And that was because, she said, she had lost my phone number or because, she said, she could never find the Sacramento Center supervisor to ask him if he had it or because she hung up if anyone but me answered or because she decided I wasn't home if the phone was busy.

One day—for all those very reasons—she and Titi decided to walk home hand-in-hand, creep, creep, creeping the two miles down Copia Street to Louisville in the hot afternoon sun. Six o'clock and Ofe's family comes over to my house wondering why Ofe and Titi aren't home. They thought I had picked her up and I thought they had picked her up. I rushed up to Grandview Park but the Sacramento Senior Citizen's Center was locked and bolted. I pictured Ofe and Titi chopped up into little pieces in some alley—still laced together at the hands—when Big Beto who was driving around on his way either to or from picking someone up—happened to spot them near the corner of Copia and Altura and brought them home. And that incident—and the excitement it generated among her children—made it easier for Ofe to say that she couldn't go to the center anymore because I was always busy and couldn't give her a ride home—without ever referencing the fact that she could have gotten the bus if she were willing to come and go according to someone else's schedule. Or that her own son-in-law Big Beto, if he'd worked it into his busy busy schedule, could have driven her up and back quite nicely.

But really it was the bingo that ended Ofe's career as a senior gadabout. When looked at in retrospect, it seemed like Ofe had agreed to go to the center in the first place because of bingo. Maybe she liked painting saints and little Dutch girls and maybe she savored the artful dodging that came with trying to get a free lunch, but it was really bingo that she was after.

According to Ofe, you had to pay a penny for each card. And then if you got a bingo on your card, you won all the pennies that had been paid into the pot for that round. If there were a lot of people there and there usually were—you could win fifty cents, maybe even a dollar.

Well, Ofe did with bingo like she did with lunch—moved ahead on credit. She took her cards without paying. I don have no money, she'd tell the person in charge of the cards. I pay you later, she'd say lightly—because she had no intention of paying. What was a penny? She had to save all hers just to buy a pack of cigarettes. When she'd win on her free cards, she'd go collect the kitty. But she'd never pay up—she couldn't remember how many cards she'd taken anyway!

Well, this went on for a little while. The women—naturally—had their collective eye upon her—and one day, they called her on it. She got a bingo and the lady in charge of the kitty—she'd had enough!—wouldn't let Ofe collect.

This made Ofe mad. Why not? she wanted to know.

Because you didn't pay for your card, the woman told her, tapping the table with her finger.

I pay for my card, Ofe insisted.

No you didn't, the lady insisted back. She knew, she'd been watching. I did, Ofe said. And then, in a sudden burst of antagonism, she called the lady one of those cruel curse words that Gilbert and his friends when they are drinking fling about with such abandon.

And the lady was horrified, and gathered all her friends around to witness Ofe's abuse. And then Ofe called them all the same thing she had called the first lady and the supervisor, that poor man, hearing the fight, rushed over to get them to come to an agreement, but neither side was willing to give in, not an inch.

Understand, these weren't big stakes—pennies, a dollar at the very most if there happened to be 100 people paying into the pot. Unless you consider—like maybe Ofe does—that triumphing over the ladies at the Sacramento Center, even at the cost of cheating—which in Ofe's book doesn't count for much—was a prize worth shooting for.

And so she quit. Or they told her to leave. One or the other—same result.

And instead she sits on her front porch from early in the morning until late at night, staring at the street, watching us all pass by.

# Rochelle Cashdan

## Rescuers

At least the Professor called early and said nothing obscene.

When the phone rang, I was at the fireplace adding kindling. I couldn't place the man's voice for a moment, but then I did. It was Professor Kelner, a distinguished scholar in my field who had written the definitive book on the Cold River people. My former field, I should say, now that my Ph.D. dead-ended me into a job doing data entry. I knew Professor Kelner all too well, but we had talked by phone only once or twice.

He was in my city calling from the train station. "I am frightened," he said flatly. "Somehow I am here. I don't know what to do."

I remembered hearing his wife had died during the past year. When I expressed my sympathy, he was quiet.

I was the one who broke the silence. "Why are you calling me?" coming down hard on the last word. I knew he had a daughter in the city who worked at the Art Museum.

"I remembered you came to the ceremony for my book that didn't win the prize."

It was true. I had seen him there and even supported his illusion that the book might win. I respected the Professor's early work, but knowing the title of the new book, I felt pleasantly sure the judges would think its theme too narrow.

Kelner had given me a hard time when he chaired my dissertation committee. After two years that culminated in an ad hoc grilling by the committee, I went looking for another chairman.

Even without the session he arranged exposing all my weak areas, I was ready to switch. In the department, people were talking about his student who quit to take a job with the city after eight years of hanging on. If I took that long, I would be ancient.

But I also remembered the Professor's book on the Cold River people. Even though Kelner was a despot in the halls of Breyer, care and humanity infused each page of history he wrote.

"I am surprised to hear from you, Professor Kelner," I said formally. I could hear him suck in his breath at the other end of the line.

"Oh, yes," he said. "Thank you for telling me."

I was silent. Finally I said, "Professor, are you still there?"

"Yes, I am here."

"I will come for you and we will decide what to do."

"I would be very grateful," he said with a dignity I recognized.

"Are you in the waiting room or in the little café?"

"The café is closed. I'll be here in the waiting room," he said soberly. He sounded close to tears.

I put on my rain jacket and pulled out the waterproof scarf I keep in a pocket. Driving to the train station took twenty minutes, which I used to brood about my broken dreams instead of making a plan for the present.

I had no trouble finding the Professor, who was the only person sitting on the benches. He must have taken a while thinking who to call. Or maybe I wasn't the first person he had tried.

"Here I am," I said, my daughterly tone galling me. ""I'll go to see when you can catch a train to take you back."

"Take me back," he said. "Where?"

"Home," I said.

"Oh," he responded. "I wish I could remember the address."

Before I walked over to the counter, I told him to stay where he was.

There was no train to Cascadia until the next morning.

"You must be ready for something to eat," I said. "We can figure out what to do at my apartment."

In the car, I asked the Professor about his daughter who worked at the Art Museum. He repeated my question vaguely. Clearly he didn't remember. I did, that's the kind of sticky mind I have, full of random mental post-it notes.

By the time we pulled up, I was determined.

This time the Professor was a gentleman as well as a scholar, holding the door open for me to go in first. I helped him off with his coat, then went into my little kitchen to make him a sandwich from what was left of a barbecued chicken. He was sitting by the fire when I came back with two cups of hot tea along with the sandwich.

He ate heartily and asked for a napkin. I brought him one and returned to sipping my tea. "Professor Kelner," I said, "I don't know whether you heard I worked a year for the Chippewa."

"That's fine," he said, and continued sipping.

I told him I was going to call Sally.

"Sally," he said thoughtfully, looking into his teacup.

"Your daughter."

"I don't remember," he said.

"You don't?" I could feel butterflies in my stomach the way I had when I was a child.

I went over to the drawer where I keep the phone book. Yes, S Kelner was listed, no address. I dialed the number, but reached his daughter's answering machine. I didn't leave a message. Tonight was the problem.

The thought of the Professor, disoriented, prowling in my apartment after I went to bed, kept my stomach churning. Besides, to my dismay, his bald head and small mustache reminded me of my father. For a minute, I stopped calculating the balance of respect and resentment due him, seeing him only as elderly and almost related. But then I started to wonder if, while he sat by the fire in my living room, he was looking on me as a deserter from our holy task. And then, another shift. Even if he remembered humiliating me and wanted to make up for it, he could never return the months and years I wasted at his pleasure.

While I was stalling, trying to think of a way to get him to leave, I managed to ask if he would like more tea.

"Yes," he said quietly.

"Haida," he was saying, on my return. Then after the tribe, he named the artist who had done the print hanging on the wall that separated my living room from the kitchen.

"Yes," I said. I had been an unwilling captive in the Professor's late afternoon class about what the catalog still called Primitive Art, but a few months later, I had fallen in love with the red and black print on tan paper and bought it. The Professor's droning lecture voice had not been his strong point, but now his tone was appreciative. Unexpectedly, I felt as if someone was troubling to knit my fragmented life together.

"Where is the bathroom?" he asked, standing up.

"Through the arch and to the right," I said, waving my hand. A few seconds later, I heard his footsteps stop. I had to follow him to show him which door.

While I watched the flames, I was still feeling queasy. I could have been back at the cozy bar near the Rez with two friends from the tribe. The men had a great time that cold, rainy night but I took sick on the cheap white wine. Professor Kelner had probably done better over the years he did his research.

Ah, ha. There were Cold River people living in the city. All I had to do was find out who was here now, not on the Rez. I went over to the phone book and began looking for names as they came into my mind. After a half dozen false starts, I found Liza Blackwater's listing.

"Ellen," she said, knowing my voice although we hadn't talked for a half dozen years.

"It's about Professor Kelner," I said, feeling embarrassed. Liza had been a friend and I hadn't done my part to keep it up.

"Is he all right?" she asked, coming right to the point.

"Yes and no," I said. "He's confused. He doesn't even remember he has a daughter here."

"Poor man," she said in her throaty voice.

"Liza, will you help?" I asked. "I don't have room and, well, he made my life hard."

"I'll come for him," she said softly. I told her where I lived.

Within half an hour she was at my place. "Burton. Ellen," she said, "It's good to see you both."

"Liza, it's good to see you," said the Professor and I, nearly in chorus.

I offered Liza a cup of tea or a glass of wine, but although she thanked me, she said it was late.

When I brought the Professor's coat, I saw Liza gazing at the print of two old Jewish scholars poring over a book.

"Which one is your grandfather?" she asked, her eyes on the wall.

"They were my grandfather's cousins," I said, which wasn't far from the truth.

I had the feeling she was ready to scold me but wouldn't in front of Burton Kelner. Instead, she put her hand on his shoulder to steady him as they walked toward the door.

# Tania Casselle

## The Trials Of Summer

Ellen didn't mind the mosquitoes but she did mind all the people that turned up on her doorstep wanting to be fed. Her husband invited them over every Friday through July and August. He said it was a barbecue, and of course he manned the barbecue, because it was a man's job, barbecuing, and therefore he said Ellen didn't have to do anything, and therefore Ellen couldn't complain at the fact that he'd invited all these people over.

People that she'd never met and never wanted to meet. People that she had met and didn't want to meet again. People that she'd met and quite liked, but not enough to have them traipsing through her hall every Friday night, their dusty shoes dirtying the carpet.

And although Tom took charge of the barbecue, flaming it up like a Viking funeral ship, throwing on steaks with slashings of red sauce and tipping the steaks onto paper plates, although Tom did all that, which he called cooking, it was still down to Ellen to buy the damn steaks and paper plates, mix the salad, clean the hall carpet, and make sure there was enough toilet paper in the downstairs bathroom. None of this counted as cooking, so she couldn't complain.

She also bought the beer and wine, made sure it was chilled beforehand, washed out the wine glasses afterwards, tidied up the sitting room for coffee after sunset, and ran around the garden with a black plastic bag in the dusk picking up discarded paper plates smeared with steak blood and honey mustard dressing. The day after, she cleaned out the barbecue pan, more cow juice burnt into metal. But as Tom was cooking, she couldn't complain. After all, how many husbands take responsibility for the meal when guests come?

There were guests with too small shorts on too large stomachs. There were guests with too loud voices for too small opinions. There were guests who brought their mistresses, and guests who brought their dogs. (Paw prints on the hall carpet, thought Ellen). There were guests who were vegetarians, so Ellen had to whisk up an omelet in the kitchen, watched by the vegetarians' thin pale faces as they insisted that she used only free-range eggs. There were guests who were important and guests who were padding. Tom's boss was important, and Ellen knew him, he had a face pink as bacon and a laugh like a donkey, but some of the important people she didn't know, and would clean their plates away into the black plastic bag too soon while Tom glared at her. There were guests who had summer houses in the Hamptons, and Ellen only had the vaguest idea of where the Hamptons were, but she tried anyway and asked them if sunrise came earlier there and whether the maids were any good?

There were guests who smoked cigars smelling of dead bodies and guests who reminded her of her mother and guests who all looked the same. When every guest had gone home, Tom looked at her, or not so much at her as just past her, over her shoulder to the still-smoldering barbecue outside.

"There," he said. "That was easy, wasn't it?"

# Avital Gad Cykman

## Soap

Little bursts of laughter explode between the twin couches and around the table. I didn't clean after last night's visit. Crumbs of salt crackers and laughter still roll over my floor.

The laughing sound does not belong here.

Long ago I left home while the family was watching TV. They didn't even notice. I closed the door on the fake TV laughter. When I called a week later, my mother asked if I'd be back in time for *Soap*.

I imagined my father and my mother falling in love and then buying a TV set to pass the years.

Ever since, I have stood on the beach every morning and looked at the passing clouds carrying light from my sea to cities that have no ocean. My ears have held the sound of the waves the way seashells do.

People used to tire me.

I was wary of the family visit as I arranged the plates, the silverware, the wine and the water glasses in the order I place them for myself, but for fifteen people.

My family seemed oversized, because the news about each newborn had skipped me. News floats like clouds, and if you sleep you miss it.

We made a toast to happiness. When the cheers dissolved into idle noise, I asked my family to be quiet for a moment and listen. We heard the permanent humming that rises beyond the silence.

"What a buzz," my cousin said.

"People say it's the voice of the universe," said my sister. "Do people talk about it?"

I wondered. I thought they were busy watching TV.

"Please fill my glass," my mother asked. She smiled. "How would you know about conversations?"

My father touched my arm.

My sister's baby cried and she got up. Babbling and mumbling erupted from the corner where she changed his diapers. My brother talked about a new TV series and teased his wife. She told me, "You really should buy yourself a television."

Before I replied, my uncle said he'd brought his.

They sat on the twin couches and joined their laughter with the TV's canned one. I imagined they saw me on the screen.

"Go back to the table," I said from the TV's belly.

"Stay with me," a stunning blond man told me. I realized he was my lover for the series.

He kissed me hard. The family held their breaths. I slapped him, because I was surprised.

The laughter burst from all sides. I did not stay with him long enough to see what followed.

My niece chased after my cousin.

"Pass the salt," my father asked. He hummed an old song from a movie.

I felt their cheer, refreshing like the salty spray of a broken wave.

Today I take a bath, and bits of laughter burst out of the water. I try to touch them, but they slip between my fingers.

# Jesse Dorris

## The Alabama Station

She found the instructions, smudged and crumpled in her backpack, another reason to run:

*1. Keep a journal for a short period of time. On one side of each page, keep a factual account of your life during that period. On the other side, try to describe what the life was like. Then write a paper describing the differences you see between the two versions.*

It was almost her last day there. The farm's grass was burned brown and she kept seeing anthills pop up between her feet as she ran, trying not to stumble too much, down towards the lake. Granny had been stuttering as she told the stories during lunch, and Leila broke a sweat trying to keep her eyes from going in and out of focus on the checkered plastic tablecloth. Grandpa poured ice tea, glass after glass, and the sugar buzzed through her like fireflies; grilled cheese sandwiches and tomato soup from a can even though it was ninety-five degrees out. "Your mom c-c-can't hide up there forever," Granny finished, and Leila took the cue to escape.

The sweat collected in her shirt as she ran. She could already feel the difference in the air down here, closer to the lake. Bees from a neighboring hive buzzed faintly. They sounded like the night when an electrical wire fell from its post outside her mom's apartment. Leila spent that night listening to it hum. Brooklyn was like that, weird noises always everywhere. But the memory of the hum sounded less and less like bees the more she thought of it. She kept running.

2. *What are some lives that seem to you potentially worthwhile subjects for biography? Why? What is your relation to the subject? Given your relation to the subject, and given the fact that biography seeks a public audience, what can you say about the kind of biography that would have to be written?*

Soon she was at the bank of the lake, and the air really was damper and less sort of solid than it was on top of the hill. She was amazed that running for a few minutes could make such a difference out here in the middle of nowhere. Last night she climbed up to the roof of her grandparents' house. You could get there from the back porch, just climb up the lattice and watch for rotten planks. The farmhouse sat on top of a hill, so on the roof she could practically see all of Alabama, with dozens of yellow stars above her. "The roof's not sturdy, won't support a girl's big as you," her grandpa said. But she sat there, safe, swatting mosquitos and watching for cars on the dirt roads spinning around the property. Two, maybe three passed the whole night. She kept thinking where is everybody, why isn't anybody going anywhere? Or are they all just watching like me? She decided next time she'd bring a flashlight, maybe she could signal someone.

One night her mom brought her to the Promenade. This was right when they'd first moved to Brooklyn. Mom showed her the city skyline and told her how every light she saw corresponded to someone: a car, an apartment, a streetlight someone built and someone repairs. Here in Alabama she could sit on a roof for hours and not see any light but the stars. "The south the south, I hate it," her mom said, "all that empty space. All the people just going through their lives and not ever seeing a soul who's not family. You'd think your grandparents would get so tired, living like that." But they didn't seem tired, Grandpa riding his tractor twice a week even with the glaucoma and bad back and arthritis. And Granny read her mystery novels and, Mom said, was Clinically Depressed, and cooked and kept the house spotless and told the same stories over and over when she couldn't remember Leila's name.

3. *Find some documents of your past life—old letters you wrote and received, transcripts, notes, papers—and use these documents as a point of departure for a description of what life was like then. Do the documents surprise you in any way? How confident are you that you know now what life was like then?*

This was the second time she'd visited, the second summer in a row, so the novelty of cows and opossums had faded a little. It was starting to feel less like a visit and more like she was just flipping between parallel lives, like each one went on separately without her realizing it. She was soaking wet now and wiped her forehead with the faded blue T-shirt from Camp Winnachuck. It's like, what if she were just changing channels, the Alabama Station to the Brooklyn Station, if the whole world really was just like cable and you could go back and forth like that. It'd be pretty cool.

Pretty stupid. This is why the kids rag on me, she thought, I say stuff like what if life's just like cable. Blech. She looked around. Her mouth felt greasy from the sandwich. She sat down right where the ground got muddy—washing her jeans would give her something to do tonight. The lake was deep green and covered with algea and little bits of wood. She had fished it, once, her and Grandpa in his rickety old boat that she kept imagining holes in. He caught a large spotted fish in between stories of the War, and it flopped on the boat's floor as it died. They had been out there since dawn and she wanted to go inside and eat lunch, maybe take a nap. But Grandpa could spend a whole day in the boat, easy. Eventually Leila stopped baiting her hook and just cast into the water, letting the line sink down to the bottom of the lake as gently as possible so the fish wouldn't notice.

*4. Many people at some point (often when it seems almost too late) develop an interest in the lives of their immediate ancestors. Write a biographical sketch of a relative. After you have begun the work, you might arrange to meet in groups with others doing the same kind of work to discuss the problems you are having collecting information, achieving the necessary detachment, developing the necessary imaginative sympathy, and making your tale interesting to an audience beyond those immediately involved with the life.*

Her mom had insisted she spent a few weeks there. Her grandparents were getting old and all that. Not that she would join her; Mom didn't really get along with her parents. Being around the three of them was like being in the boat: a few hours of boredom interrupted by sharp fears of sinking. Would it have been worse to refuse and be in Brooklyn for the summer? She threw a stone into the lake and listened for the plop. Ripples edged out towards the mud. A guilt trip from Mom would have been inevitable, and also spending every day trapped in the apartment because she was too freaked out to let Leila explore the city alone. Her friends were at camp or working at their parents' stores. She would have read a lot of books, watched too much TV, not much of a vacation really. But it might have been better than just killing time here, putting up with her grandparents because they weren't dead yet.

Ouch. She didn't mean that, she thought. Boredom and heat were making her cranky. She got up and walked around the lake for a while. A big log was slowly sinking into the mud, its bottom end a deeper brown than the top. Bits of it floated around like desert islands. "Remember the time," Granny had said during lunch, "when you kept calling Hawaii a dessert island? There wasn't a thing to convince you that you could be wrong." Leila stared at her grandmother and wished that every time she remembered something it wasn't some kind of put-down. She kicked the log and another inch sank into the mud, water sucking and rolling up to the surface.

*5. What kind of person would you most want to be like? Is this person fictional or real? How do you know? What do you expect to happen, what kind of person do you expect or hope to be later? Try to write so as to let yourself and your reader participate imaginatively in the lives you describe.*

A cloud of mosquitos appeared, the lake must be drying up. In the boat, Grandpa tried to explain how you can tell the depth of a lake by the number of mosquitos around it—the more there are, the less deep. So she should quit complaining about being bit and start realizing this lake won't be here much longer. So how come there aren't any mosquitos in the city, she asked, there's not much water in the ponds there? That's not water, that's trash, he shot back and cast out his rod.

She sniffed her arms to make sure she hadn't sweated the insect repellant off. Her skin smelled like coconuts, salt, and tomato soup. She wasn't sure what the mosquitos would make of that. How long had she been out there? A few hours, probably, because the sun was pretty low in the sky. Grandpa's hosing down the patio, Granny wants to know what to make for dinner. Chores and food. She could call her mom later, if she wanted to, or not. Grandpa would tell some stories about when they lived in Alaska or Kansas, or try to get information about her mom. She would put a sweater on when it got dark and the heat burnt off.

Granny would ask if she wanted to play c-c-cards or p-p-put a p-puzzle together. The three of them would eat dinner and go to bed, suddenly realizing how tired they all were, Leila listening at the door for a chance to escape.

That night, after the dishes were put away and the hum of the washing machines replaced the hum of the dishwasher, Leila sat on the couch and waited for them to fall asleep. Granny's hands were trembling over a half-finished puzzle, little puppy heads making their way through the ripped, dog-eared cardboard pieces. Grandpa was watching golf and every few minutes his neck would jerk as he woke up. An hour passed that felt longer than any of her last twelve. She thought of the flashlight tucked under her pillow, ready for her to grab and take to the roof. Goosebumps rushed over her as the air conditioner came on. Granny had brought her mom up six times during dinner, pretending each time she had forgotten the last, but Leila said nothing. On the couch was a thin blue blanket Granny's grandma had made, and she wrapped it around her as she waited.

Finally granpa grumbled and limped his way past her down the long hallway to the bedroom. Granny sighed and pressed another piece into place. "Don't be up all night, hear?" Leila smiled and she lied, no I'll be in bed soon, and tried not to gag at the lavender perfume as granny kissed her cheek.

*6. Read two accounts of the same person by two different people. What differences do you see? Set these differences out as specifically as you can. How do you account for the differences? Are they a matter of one person's greater knowledge of the facts or of a particular bias? How can you compromise, collate, and consolidate these accounts to arrive at a third portrait of the subject?*

The heat on the roof was amazing. She couldn't understand how it could be so much colder inside, she knew a little about freon and all that but it still didn't make sense that just like four feet away the world could be so different. Just like down at the lake, all these worlds together. She made her way to the flat part where the two sides of the tar roof met and thought about this one day out on the boat when Grandpa gutted a fish right in front of her. He said something about just 'cause she's a girl she should still know something about blood and guts, to not be like her mother. The fish had the same color eyes as this weird girl in her Geometry class last year who always had her hands covering her mouth. Leila tried to talk to her a couple times but never really managed to say anything, she'd always get too nervous 'cause the girl never said anything back, to anyone ever, and Leila would break out into a sweat and have to run into the bathroom. Just thinking about the girl now made her almost loose her footing on the roof and she had to get onto her knees to keep from falling.

What was going on in Brooklyn? Was her mom passed out right now, her empty wine bottle on the floor next to her? Was it this hot there? Were the mosquitos bad? It felt like she had never even been to Brooklyn, two weeks here and New York was like a movie. She knew in a couple days she'd feel the way about Alabama, the yellow stars and the logs and the boat. It was like this last summer too. She reached the top of the roof, her knees burning from the crawl, and straddled the edge.

Somewhere a dog barked. No cars were on the roads. Something that felt like a bug crawled over her thigh, and the sound of her slap echoed into the fields. Why was she thinking about that girl right now? The worst part about getting older was not being able to understand why she thought about the things she did. And how she couldn't talk to anyone about it—the other girls at school just wanted to talk about boys or what cup size they wore or who was the bigger slut, or that weird girl in the corner who never said anything. Her mom would just groan and say you think you're old. Leila sighed and tried not to notice how much it sounded like granny's sigh back in the living room.

*7. Using the journal or the documents you've collected, write a description of "the person to whom these things happened." Who is that person in relation to the person now writing?*

Leila dug in her pockets for the small rubber flashlight. Turning it on, she passed the weak circle of light over the fields and wondered if it would reach the road on the other side of the fence. It didn't, but it was still the brightest thing other than the stars that she could see. She made a figure eight, the grass looking burned in the weak light. She turned it on and off a couple times, trying to make the light strobe, but it just looked like someone turning a flashlight on and off as fast as she could. Leila lay back, anchoring the roof between her thighs, and shined the light up into the sky. Thousands of stars lit the sky, mocking the white light she shined back. In Brooklyn you never see stars, that's how bright the city is. But so what. She sat up, trying to figure out the first thing she'd do when she got back, but all she could think of was how to lie to her mom, the perfect way to tell her she had a good enough time that maybe she wouldn't have to come back next summer. And no, Granny and Grandpa didn't ask about her.

She shined the flashlight into the trees in front of her. They surrounded the fields around the lake, but for some reason she had never explored them. She bent forward, trying to get the light deeper into the forest, but all she could see was bark. She sighed and turned off the light.

*8. Have you read one of the many fictional works that have been written as if they were biographies? What difference do you see between that fictional work and a true biography? How do you account for these differences?*

But the light was still there. A little brighter, even. It was like a reflection, except her flashlight wasn't on. The leaves were lit up like Christmas lights, their bark brown and glossy. Little shards of light broke through onto the grass, criss-crossing and slowly reaching out towards the house. The light grew from a pin-point into a small circle, bisected like a geometry problem by the tree trunks, as it began to move up towards the roof. Leila counted the seconds until it reached her, paralyzed, her legs burning from the heat of the tar roof. It was a spotlight. Somewhere a car honked its horn, and the sound fell over the insects buzzing and dogs barking as the light grew brighter, and then the sounds died and she could hear feet crushing the burnt grass. And as the light hit the edge of the roof and began to touch her legs, Leila leaned forward as far as she could, out over the roof and onto the fields below, and the light flashed a few times as she saw the small outline of a body walking towards the house.

    The shock forced Leila off the roof in half the time it took to get up there. Sliding down one side, she felt pieces of skin scrape off. She jumped from the bottom of the roof to the ground and crumpled, grass pricking the back of her neck and cooling her legs. She raised her head and looked around for her flashlight, but it was gone. And the other light was gone too, like someone had put a hand over it, and there was only the sound of insects. That girl's name was Sandy, their moms knew each other. What was she doing right now? Leila closed her eyes and pictured her lying in bed, the grass becoming pillows and sheets, and there were no cars on the roads here, no alarm clocks or remote controls to tell them where they were. Her legs began to ache from the fall, and they jerked a little as she lay there, they flopped like she was trying to swim instead of falling asleep here, mosquitos ready to bite. She'd never come back, she'd never tell her mom a thing.

*9. Looking back, what are the big moments, the milestones, in your life? Do you perceive any "movement," any direction in them? Have you changed your idea of what the big moments in your life were? How did this happen? Has your sense of the direction of your life changed? Do you expect it to change any more? How?*

# Hugh Fox

## Genealogy

1.

Old once white, ten percent dissolved wood farmhouse on the edge of an unpaved road, up, up, they always had to be up, porch and out-buildings in back, a shabby dismantling barn, perfect albeit antique silo.

"So this is it," said Jerry, the country-know-it-all guide, "I don't wanna try to drive away ... you never know ... look around if you want, half an hour and then we can go back into town, we've got another hour and twenty minutes before sundown, and dusk lingers out here...."

The former farm fields, stubble remnants of old corn, apple trees with half-mature apples on them. No broken windows, the roof still kind of shambley but intact.

"You can just leave, I'm staying overnight."

"Listen," hesitating, weak and wobbly for a moment, and then bayonetish stuff, "I just can't let you out here like this. It's dangerous, there's animals, like black bears, coyotes ... you never know.... I've seen porcupines."

Pat reaches into his pocket. A hundred-dollar bill. Hands it to the driver.

"Even worse ... bribes.... I don't say this place belongs to anyone any more, but...," but the driver still takes it, acts like he doesn't want to, "the

2.

first time in thirty years I've seen a hundred dollar bill. So what are you gonna do tonight, what about food? You know...."

"I've got some stuff in my pockets."

"Well ..." And he backs away slowly, reluctantly, goes to his ancient, constantly-being-fixed Ford, stops with a certain medieval solemnity. "So when do I pick you up?"

Sam takes out his cell-phone, points to it.

"Á bientot!"

"Whatever! I suppose I'm supposed to be impressed, but I'm more de- than im- ... I trust all will go well. You'll end up with the birds in the old cornfields looking for one last kernel. Although I think even that's stopped fifty years ago."

"Of uncommon sense."

One last sigh that says impatience, he's a real patient and needs HELP, HELP, HELP ... and he's off and gone, Sam wondering if he even put on his safety belt.

"Ah, well ..."

Up to the front door. Locked. Curtains still on the windows, but he can see wooden columns inside, always loved/loves wooden columns in entrance ways, between rooms, down the sagging wood steps amazingly well-preserved, always loving old/ancient concrete block houses out in

3.

the middle of nowhere like here, the blocks as unalterable as the ancient pyramids in the Andes, everything else, wood, plastic, synthetic all mortal, but concrete blocks immortal. Around the side of the house to the back, down to the basement door, not expecting it to be open, all decided to break in if it wouldn't open, but ... eins, zwei, drei and he was in.

Stench. The stench of old wood, old walls, almost like old tobacco, like the stuff he used to (pipe) smoke, cockroaches, one small mouse.

"Hey, don't run away, I'm as harmless as a cigar butt."

But it was 1,2,3 gone. He hadn't seen a cigar butt (or pipe) in years, what had ever happened to macho cigars?

Tables, workbenches, scythes, rakes, saws, huge "snipers," watering cans, old iron wheels over against one wall, walking through the basement past piles of old clothes, huge chests, not like his place, all books and computers, walking up creaky stairs to the living room, a sofa, family photos, into the kitchen, an old sloppily-fluffy-haired woman in a long blue-jeanish dress, squinting blue eyes.

"Yeah, your nose is telling the truth, potato dumplings and chicken hearts, gizzards, liver, kidneys, all the good parts ground up into a guess-what-I-am delight. My specialty, you remember, come on in, me boy, you're looking … I was going to say old, but…," laughing, hugging

4.

him, feeling it, but was sure something was wrong with his eyes, all those heart and prostate-cancer pills … "I used to kind of hate winter, you know, nothing to do. But nowadays, I don't care, there's Sammy the dog, he's outside wandering around right now, but in the winter he's inside most of the time. And I love fireplaces and watching Al start the fires. I start things up once in a while. We miss Ireland, but …"

A tall guy wearing a felt cowboy hat, suspenders, farm jeans, comes in, gives him another hug, as if he were feeling it, seeing it, hearing it.

"So I'm glad you could make it. Homestead instead of no-stead," laughing, yet another hug, "Whatever that means … good corn crop this year, and potatoes. No famines here, and wait until you see the pigs, gotta do some smoking pretty soon, but we're set for a long, long winter, and the deer, there's always the deer, the wild turkeys, grouse. I hate the migratory species that desert us every winter."

"So fancy, 'migratory species'!" his mother ridicules him.

"I read a lot, especially in the winter, that's all I learned to do was to read, but … there's country fairs, good book-deals…," motioning for Pat to follow him into the living room, the shelves filled with books, hard-covers, fancy, for a moment feeling he was in some sort of palatial library.…

"Why did you ever decide to homestead?"

5.
"It was like going back …"
"Back?"
"Erin go Bragh.…"
"I'm afraid I never …"
"Imagine pre-English Ireland, pre-English Scotland, Wales. English history is such a …"

Suddenly a bunch of little girls and guys coming in and all dressed like the nineteenth century, long dresses, short pants, wearing little white inverted cupcake container hats over quakerish, shakerish long hair, like he'd suddenly walked through a time-barrier he'd always wanted to walk through, back to sanity.

"Come on out, let's go out, you're got to see the mules.…"
"And horses."
"The smelly cows."
"Smellier pigs."

Everyone laughing, off in the distance the Montana mountains you could see through the windows.

"Go ahead, no problem, we'll save supper for you all," says Kitchen Grandma.

"Enjoy it while you can!" Mr. Emperor-Farmer of it all, "you ought to see the winter here … but I love it too, the fireplace and everything outside

6.

white, rows of corn stubble, like you've never seen sun before … and I still go hunting.…"

"Come on! Come on!"

The kiddies screaming, Pat trying to figure out who belonged to him, all the brothers and sisters and kids and grandkids, cousins …

Wavering as he goes out, as if he'd never seen the sky before, a pond in back of the house, endless forests, almost expecting Indians, wouldn't have been surprised if King Solomon walked out of the woods, King Solomon or The Trinity descending, a diamond triangle descending out of the sky, one of the little blondies scream-asking, "So how do you like it?"

"I …"

No words, like he'd never seen clouds before, and a deer off on the edge of the forest.

"I …"

Turning around and then back around and they began to thin out into clouds, mist, their voices becoming thrushes and crows, no more smoke coming out of the chimney, their mist hands waving goodbye and their mist faces sad with loss, back up to the house, empty, no one, no smells, voices,

In the beginning there was nothing and nothing became everything

7.
and everything cloud-rained away, down the rivers into the sea of irreversibility.

# Anne Germanacos

## SAYING I LOVE YOU IN A VARIETY OF WAYS

Teeth wander, chomp relentlessly, eat their own neighboring flesh.

\*

(She files for divorce because he stepped on her clothes?)

\*

A mother may be the extra padding a person needs. She may bundle you, snowsuit in hot sun, she may leave you naked out in the cold.

\*

A mind can organize a festival, it can set up a fair.

\*

(Engage the sweet spot, time's carburetor.)

\*

The clouds stole her breath.

\*

(Opening the vent brought up the flame.)

\*

sentences occur

(heavenly and organized)

\*

Try to dwell elsewhere: amongst and between, inside (and out)

\*

ancient walls, pecking chickens

\*

"pergamenon" or parchment

\*

There's a soft spot where the Hebrew *daka* becomes the Arabic *dawquika*—that sound in the middle so subtle it almost evades hearing.

\*

A lie, it's true, requires a liar.

\*

Do I address a you without quite calling it you?

\*

(Sometimes need to go through oneself to get to the other side.)

\*

A cockroach leg with its feathery spikiness and that thread-thin part, attached.

\*

with the ease of breath or laughter

\*

(Occasionally still long for an island with a definite perimeter, limits outlined in shore.)

\*

Those sheep lips, always about to utter something incomprehensible.

\*

Pythagoras: Stay silent or say something better than silence.

\*

We saw dawn arrive.

\*

In other words, no longer requiring space between the peas, potatoes, and meat.

\*

Make yourself scarce, invite others in.

\*

The rats are back!

\*

The world was unbearably close and apparently forever.

\*

What would a Chorus be saying at the edges of her pages?

\*

*Interpret me.*

\*

Courting time's arrest in various poses.

\*

Still at large.

\*

A rat paces, but almost inaudibly.

\*

*The only real point is to be alive, obvious as that may seem.*

\*

A black goat stands tall like a man, front legs its arms, untangling the knot of carob branch, taking its pick.

\*

It's spring—she's cleaning.

\*

(You make an omelette of the relatives that feel like leftovers.)

\*

Walking through sheep: They'll go around you—fast!—in one or two streams, as if you're a rock in the river of them.

\*

In the unknown zone, questing.

\*

He sits, moves his limbs within the distinct circumference of the space they displace.

*

(It could shine up nicely.)

*

Fog is different from cloud and haze is another thing entirely.

*

(I hear the birds. Do they hear me?)

*

When the weight goes out of words, just puffs.

*

Maybe none of the women dance that circle anymore.
Maybe it's an ancient figment of imagination.

But I saw it once, I swear I held their hands.

*

suffering, but not so much that you can't walk it back around to joy

*

In thrall to chaos?

*

Trying to keep the color within the lines.

*

(Days when words aren't the friends you thought they were.)

\*

Those three red flowers—bright, expansive, wide open.
Role models.

\*

I can write letters to people in far-away places, even, in some sense, to my mother, though it would only ever reach the her in me.

\*

The earth swings us round.

\*

Resuming life.
(interrupted)

\*

Church bells ring at quarter past four, the second Friday of Lent.

\*

Open to the wind, this house smells like Easter.

\*

When sobs calm.
*Who hasn't been there?*

\*

Mothers, interpreters of fathers. *Translators?*

\*

The virtue of speechlessness? *The usefulness.*

*

Sitting by the fire, she asked: Is that your stomach or the rat?

*

(Some of us are homesick before we've ever left home.)

*

A body has its secrets, its codes. It may take a while to find the decoder—nothing you'll find in a cereal box.

*

Drinking black tea. What the hell.

*

(Nose your way through disorder, cultivate it.)

*

One feels it behind the ribs, a space large enough to prance in.

*

Trying to see clearly what she sees faintly.

*

(Heat alters the days. You're still wearing wool.)

*

Nietzsche: "Those Greeks were superficial—out of profundity."

*

Another cockroach leg dangling.
Kafka or coincidence?

(contradictory, polysemic)

*

Nothing forever, nothing always.
(Something sometimes and everything once in a while.)

*

Conflicting perspectives, clashing reconciliations.

*

Rainbows irradiate vapor. They rarely light the way.

*

Stirred into a configuration: soupy, stewed, corrupt, and tasty.

*

(Sitting with infinity, trembling.)

*

Skin: parchment.
(your skin, my parchment)

*

Birds make off with our hair.

*

This, after all, is what you do, with the tip of a knife, day after day.

\*

Cunt.
A better word, less blunt?

\*

We clink together for health, sometimes tapping faultlines.

\*

A sister may be the very closest you'll ever get to God.
She knows you backwards and forwards.

You tremble before her gaze, spout conciliatory nonsense, and pray to her in shiny mirrors.

\*

Many small, not-exactly-interchangeable parts.

\*

She says: It's losing a mother.

\*

The cats continue to gambol; the rats are silent.

\*

Please teach me to pronounce the difficult letters, especially the breathy *h*.

\*

Midwife?
(butcher)

\*

Joseph Brodsky: "A real history of consciousness starts with one's first lie."

\*

Broken to bits, the bits take shape.
(You aim to stay broken, in bits, all potential.)

\*

It takes forty gallons of maple sap to make one of syrup.

\*

Do dead tongues ever come back to life?

\*

(Those dancing hawks—a pair.)

\*

English, a sea.

\*

The sacred thing the culture forgot.

\*

knocking on wood, spitting out the evil eye

\*

I love the smell of sheep: part lanolin, part dung.

\*

Lakoff: "To change the concept of *category* is to change our understanding of the world."

\*

I go past animal, human, then get stuck on my sister's penis.

\*

(Those red bugs, tail to tail: just like us.)

\*

But think of this: visible penises and invisible ones.

\*

(We go breast to penis and back again, hardly stopping for breath.)

\*

It's spring—he's tilling.

\*

Not just icon or amulet but a *real process*.
(Work on saying *I love you* in a variety of ways.)

\*

Those red bugs, tail to tail: I pick up the pair and pull them apart, trying to understand who, in this pair, is who.

\*

It's so quiet, I thought that moth's flutter was my sister.

# Terri Lee Hackman

## BUNNY-EARS

See her there.

It must be midnight in Manchester and there's a girl, about 9 years old, wearing bright pink flashing bunny-ears. She's on the sidewalk with the bus stop at her right and a row of phoneboxes behind her, all lined up, waiting for someone, anyone, to use them.

The girl shifts her weight and seems to balance for tiny moments on one foot, then the other. She glances around, and suddenly looks very serious. She looks at you and you know something's not right. But what can you do? It's the city, it's midnight, you aren't supposed to mess with kids. You could get in trouble. But she looks scared.

The bunny-ears flash and nod as she turns her head. She takes a strand of her hair and twists it, pulls it, caresses it, drags it across her lips. And she turns around, all the way around, so you get the full view of her, her pink and white and silver trainers, her brown jersey jacket with sassy pink buttons, her brand-new jeans with the brand-new patches at the ass. This is no way to dress a kid in the city at midnight.

"Hey, Little Lady, are you lost?"

Now you've done it. Now you've gone and done it. She looks away from you, turns her face away and doesn't say anything. You move closer and you can smell diesel exhaust, and expensive hair conditioner, and rot from your own mouth. You bend down to her, close enough so that if she turns toward you her smooth hair will brush your face. But she draws away, doesn't turn her head the way you'd hoped, doesn't swing her hair.

"Come here. Come here and I'll help you find your mama. I like your bunny-ears."

She looks up at you as she steps back. A big Asian guy passes by and looks at you but not as if he sees anyone. And then a slag of a woman, so skinny you cannot believe her legs can hold her up, they should buckle, in their black sheer stockings they should fold right under her, you would like to knee them, clip the ankles, see her drop and break. She's on her mobile and she's laughing and sways just a little as she tries to keep herself straight up and talking as she spikes along on her stilettos.

There's movement beside you and you look down at Bunny-Ears and she's being hugged by a woman who keeps saying 'I thought I'd lost you! Oh, I thought …' and you feel a little nauseous and a little scared. You move away from them, as if you haven't noticed them, as if you're very interested in the phone booths, at the movie posters plastered to their sides of some romantic comedy that will be here soon—a young white woman looks over her shoulder at a grinning blond man—they're lined up five in a row, looking and looking at each other.

Bunny-Ears holds her mother's hand and is crossing the street away from the bus stop, still flashing like a pink Christmas tree. You watch her until she goes around a corner somewhere where you'll never see her again, and feel a little sad because you know you would have helped her, in your own way.

# Tsipi Keller

## Spiders

Arachnologists tell us that for most species in nature, a husband's place is in the digestive tract of his wife. I know very little about nature, let alone spiders, but I do know about husbands (three so far) and stomachs. As a little girl of five, I said to my mother: "If you put a dime in my palm every time you tell me a way to a man's heart is his stomach, when I'm eighteen I'll have a nice dowry to catch him with." My mother laughed and stroked my hair and said I'd grow up to be a bookkeeper. And she was right! I work for Lilinbaum & Lilinbaum and make a good enough living, and with moneys collected from my exes and wisely invested, I'm not poor.

> As an aside, let me provide a short and relevant history: my first two exes perished under my care. The third, a mistake and a virtual cliché, eloped with a cleaning lady from Guatemala.

Still, I am not content. At moments of respite like now, I sit in the cafeteria of L&L and, over a modest lunch of greens, ponder when and how we veered off nature's path. I watch my fellow-workers (yes, most of them are fellows) in their suits and brown shoes and eat my heart out. It's silly and futile, but I can't help it. In my own small way I'm a scientist, a kind of an investigator (instigator!). I watch them and conclude: They don't look it, but they must be clever. Or, more clever than us females. For, excluding my own quite satisfying record, if anyone ends up in the digestive tract of the other, it is usually the female in the male's.

Then, just like that, it hit me: God exists! And, since He made man in His own image, He was naturally sympathetic to male issues, exhibiting a characteristic ambivalence toward females, whores and saints alike.

I sneaked a glance around me. Great revelations pulsed through me, and I wondered if their impact showed on my face. My boss was sitting at the next table, reading a pamphlet and cuddling his balls under the napkin. Ours was an open and tolerant firm, all creeds and religions were revered, and every Friday at 4 p.m., we gathered in the boardroom for a toast and a brief, open-ended prayer.

> As an aside, let me admit right here lest I forget:
> If I had balls, I'd be cuddling them too, for they
> are soft and bouncy and handy.

It was only Monday, and here I was, awash in religious awakenings. I wanted to stand up and reveal myself, share what I had just experienced, but common sense—the proverbial: "There's a time for everything"—prevailed. I finished my salad, then joined my boss for an exploratory chat. He had just divorced his wife (no one knew why), and I thought I might as well get started on number four.

# Edith Konecky

## Margo on the Beach

Warm lacy foam bubbled around Margo's ankles, bathwater-warm and so soft she barely felt it. She looked out over this emerald, semi-tropical sea, so unlike the restless cold violent New England one she had grown up with, all cold blues and blacks with wall-high, white-crested waves relentlessly piling up to crash, sweeping, surging, pushing, pulling, defiant and challenging, powerful and awesome. Hard to believe this sea and that had the same name, were one, continuations of each other. This one was a pussycat. It would be impossible to drown in it, even intentionally, which was what she was considering. You could walk out into it forever, with no jolting transition from air to water, from warm to cold, and then you could begin to swim, probably also forever. If you tired, which was unlikely, you would float, gently cradled aloft as on a mountain of tapioca pudding. No, this sea was too benign for suicide.

There are no new stories, she thought, looking down at her ankles, her legs. They were beginning to go. Her knees. The inner thighs. She was sick and tired of gravity, as relentless and unforgiving as that northern ocean. She was in her late forties. Last night, Paul had told her that he was leaving her. Even if she survived the pain of that, she was sure nobody would ever fall in love with her again.

She walked into the water and when it reached her hips, she fell back against it and lay for a while looking into the cloudless sky. They had been here two weeks, a sort of reverse honeymoon, a gallmoon. She was bored with the perfect weather, which had begun to seem not so much weather as its absence. If only men felt the same way about women, that perfection was a bloody bore. She could see Paul, now, running in the distance into her field of vision, on the final leg of his morning run, running, as they said, for his life, for his heart, for his lungs, for skin and muscle tone, for his breakfast. He was a dozen years older than she, nearing sixty, yet women even as young as his graduate students threw themselves at him, would probably seduce him on his deathbed.

She watched him increase in size and detail as he came nearer, hating him in proportion to his growing presence. He ran gracefully, his arms swinging rhythmically, his rather short legs pumping, kicking up sprays of sand, his straight dark hair flopping onto his brow. He would be bathed in sweat by now, every pore open, his heart thumping hard. She knew his body as she knew her own. It was her body. No more; he would be taking it elsewhere.

As he reached the stretch of beach where they always swam and where she now reclined, he pulled off his t-shirt without breaking stride, dropping it onto the sand, and dashed into the water, throwing up a dazzle of spume through which she could see on his face the blind concentration of one who has pushed himself to the edge of endurance. She closed her eyes and heard him thrash about, then come to rest a few yards from her, gasping. She heard the deep breaths slowly lengthen and grow more measured.

"Good morning," he said. "Or are you hung over?"
"Not at all."
"How do you do it?"
"Easily."
"Yes, too bad. You're really becoming an alcoholic, you know."
He scissor-kicked closer to her, until he was lying beside her, his leg washing against hers.
"Did you fuck him?" he asked.

"Probably. I'm not sure." The water rocked her gently. She could fall asleep if he would go away.

"Is that what will happen to you?" he said, his voice hard with contempt.

"I hope so."

She turned onto her stomach and swam away from him, back toward shore. When her toes scraped bottom, she pulled her long slender body erect. The water came only to her knees. Those knees. She walked slowly against the water toward shore. At its edge, she spied a glint of silver and bent to pick it up. It was the shell of a snail, a nautilus, about two inches long, paper-thin and nacreous, perfectly formed though no telling how long it had been emptied of its tenant. She held it toward the sun and saw rainbows shimmering in its silvered finish. How beautiful it was, and how light in her hand, the next thing to air.

Paul was right behind her., "What have you got there?" he asked. She held it up for him to see. "A nautilus," he said, reaching for it. "It's perfect." She withdrew the hand that held it. He was not to touch it.

"Let me see it," he said, impatiently.

She walked away from him, toward the fringe of coconut palms beyond which, on its rise, sat the thatch-roofed sandstone cottage they were renting. She needed a cigarette, coffee.

"I want to see the sequence," he said, coming abreast of her, holding his hand out.

She showed it to him again. "Don't touch it," she said.

He looked at her with disbelief, then smiled. "You're like a small child," he said.

The shell was a spiral, its markings delineating the chambers that had held the growing mollusk that once inhabited it. She saw that he was right, each segment was the size of the sum of the two preceding it. She had been married to Paul, a scientist, long enough to speak his language. Sometimes, she thought she spoke it even better than he, though she made her living writing soaps for television. When Paul was angry at her, which was almost always, he told her that she was no better than her own cheap characters, that she had a cheap and vulgar mind and that was why she was so successful at what she did. But she knew better. He had never been able to hurt her by impugning her intelligence, which she knew was superior even to his. Her behavior might sometimes be cheap and vulgar, but never her mind. The way to hurt her was to remind her that she was not beautiful, something her beautiful mother had so often done while she was growing up, and something Paul was doing now by having fallen in love with someone else. She knew that she was terrified. When he was gone she would be … what would she be? Who would she be?

"Yes," he said. "Fibonacci. Each segment the exact length of the two preceding it."

"I know," she said. "Perfectly measured growth."

"It's beautiful," Paul said.

"All silver and pearl."

"Please let me hold it for a minute," he pleaded.

She smiled at him. She hated him. She needed him. She held the shell, the perfect shell of the nautilus toward him and as he reached for it she crushed it in her hand, pulverized it, and let the dust of it fall into his outstretched palm.

He looked up at her in disbelief, and then not in disbelief.

"Yes," he said, nodding. "I know. I'm sorry."

# Nathan Leslie

## It Can't Hurt, Can It?

When I say "testify" I don't mean this in any traditional slash Christian sense. No baptisms or the like. Nor do I mean this in the legal sense. I simply and directly am implying a simple and direct statement testifying as to the truth-quality of my position. I don't mean to sound pretentious; I am known to be anything but.

The first thing you should be aware of is that I practice a cutting edge slash alternative form of reiki which I like to call "remote reiki." The United Federation of Touchless Touch Masters has determined that I am the second most highly ranked Reiki practitioner in the region—not that I keep an active tally or the like (these are, of course, subject to whim and this frequently shifts according to the high-drama of Reiki-whimsy; it's all political). There is an ebb and flow to such things.

This story starts and ends with remote Reiki.

It also starts and ends with Ed. Ed is my husband.

You may consider it odd for someone named Charlotte Felicity Emily Grainsborough (that's me, CFEG) to find herself betrothed to a gentleman who goes by the name of Ed, however, I would remind you that his full nomenclature is Edward Williams Williamson.

What happened over the long course of our marriage is this: though we commenced in synch in virtually every way—spiritually, emotionally, psychologically, philosophically, mentally, gastronomically, astrologically—the air slowly hissed out of the balloon of our marriage to such a degree that nine months later I wasn't so sure. Edward was identifiably exact to the man who proposed to me, tears galloping down his face as he mouthed Whitney Houston to me under a delicate gossamer array of pink and purple. Yes, perhaps his overindulgence in margaritas assisted such pathos, however, who's to say this wasn't also the emergence of his identifiably authentic self? Perhaps his true self lay dormant, ready to erupt from the normalcy of daily living.

But as my mentor likes to say, "One year is a long spell to unite with any one soul."

I miss Ed: he is still my best friend and soul mate.

That said, I additionally believe we all possess more than one soul mate. Perhaps an entire yellow school bus chock-filled with soul mates awaits each of us. And on that bus of soul mates, each soul mate frolics with the other soul mates, in wait for potential union with the soul mate who is us. Who wouldn't want a ride on *that* bus?

So there wasn't one specific moment that brought the house of marital cards tumbling down. There were many.

Ed claims, however, that the incident with Jarvis was the straw that broke his lovelorn back.

Jarvis was (and is) a client of the first order. He is what we within the reiki community call a "steadfast"—a weekly customer who sought not only a "quick fix" for his ailments, as most do, but truly a continual lifestyle alteration and improvement. Needless to say Jarvis was (and is) a highly valued reiki nook.

Which is why I saw little problem (much less a conflict of interest) with having Jarvis au naturel, privates a-jutting as I wandered my hands invisibly—close but not touching—over his protuberances. He complained of testicular numbness and overall genital disturbances unmoved by the appearance of womanly beauty. I revealed this simply and directly to Edward, but he remained stubbornly convinced that something extraordinary slash interpersonal slash quasi-erotic may have been afoot between yours truly and Mr. Jarvis.

Anything could be further from the truth.

In actuality it was the interruption Edward provided which caused the said Jarvis protrusion to wilt and caused the overall healing process to retard significantly. In other words, though my husband views Jarvis's nakedness as a sign of my cuckoldry as Philip P. Seaman Esq. has informed me, a suit in pursuance of legal damages for lost wages is not out of the question.

To wit: point seven of such a line of reasoning—my designated home office space was at the time affixed with a "Please Knock" sign, which was conveniently ignored by my husband at the moment of my so-called "indiscretion." A "Please Knock" sign is not only a request (says Philip P. Seaman Esq.), but an invisible contract between members of a residence. Willfully ignoring such a sign is a breach of unwritten contract, and such a breach in itself is worthy of damages paid in full.

Who said that hovering a healing hand above another man's erect penis and taut scrotal skin constitutes infidelity? Was there touching? Did seed emerge from such a healing state? Does the Bible make mention of legitimate and documented reiki techniques upon a wounded groin? This was a healing act related 110% to my professional acts.

Speaking of reiki, what I now realize is that the crux of the problem is this: I was stubbornly practicing reiki in person rather than taking advantage of a much larger and infinitely more lucrative *remote* reiki market. In this light, the betrayal by Edward was a helpful pointer: I realized then and there that I must sever the chains which tie me to in-person healing and instead embrace a much larger community—the world! I could constantly hover! I could be a cloud in the cloud!

As Edward stewed and worse (more on this in a moment) as a result of "the Jarvis incident," as I began calling it, I simply decided to be proactive, to take the high road (tolls need not apply).

This high road, unfortunately, involved posting ads online and sending hundreds of millions of e-mails to various addresses I had acquired over the years. I became, I suppose, a kind of spammer in my attempt to salvage my connubial relations.

By this point Ed had hunkered down at the Red Roof Inn off 216, watching horse racing and drinking beer and kicking his sad sack heart around the shabby beige industrial carpet. I still felt empathy.

"Why don't you let me try it?"

His voice was thin, almost weakened. However, it could've been the Red Roof echo-chamber. "I just need to take a few antacids, Charl."

He was in denial; the phone plastic felt cool against my neck. I could feel the emergence of positivity.

"You know, it can't hurt," I said.

"Yes, it can."

"How?"

"It can hurt my soul," he said. "Deeply. My confidence. Everything."

"I'm going to anyway," I said. I began my complex set of preparations.

"You can't forcibly reiki me," he said.

"But I can *heal* you remotely," I said. "And you won't even know it. You're still my husband, Edward."

"I'm only going by Ed now."

"Reiki isn't a verb, by the way. It's 'heal.' Heal is the action."

This was our repartee, where our relationship landed.

A few more exchanges and Edward disengaged. He muttered a sentence about needing to quash my maternal instinct, or something to this effect in his parlance.

I continued my preparations and performed my healing anyway: who says one can't compel a horse to drink from water?

By the next day his intestinal complaints had diminished (I didn't ask him about antacids then).

Post-healing I must almost always, in addition, cleanse myself. I must expunge the accumulated filth from my qi. My healing process has to do with seeking my own center, and then crawling into my own center so that my center takes the shape of a kind of nest of energy which encapsulates me in such a way that it takes on its own energy. It is only when the energy of my center-nest exceeds my own energy that I know I can return to the activities of mankind.

These activities often revolve around gustatory matters (one of the ironies of my husband's post-flight maladies). I told him that if he ingests the shell of a robin's egg along with sufficient dandelion sports this would perfectly compliment my healing gestures on his behalf. Little did he listen. My balance has to do with not just rudimentary matters as minerals and vitamins, but more or less with the tone of what I ingest. For instance, I usually find that positivity arrives with the consumption of orange foods on even-numbered days. To wit, on the 18$^{th}$ I find myself dining on clementine wedges and tangerines, carrots and saffron-spiced rice. On oddly numbered days it's blue or green, or some combination of the two—broccoli and cabbage and blueberries and avocados.

Ed was at the door three days after our healing session (whether or not he was aware of such session). Thankfully for his displaced sense of bourgeois morality I was not involved with healing male genitalia at this juncture. Frankly, the current state of the economy has put a dent in the reiki (remote or otherwise) market.

Ed clutched a handful of garbage bags.

"Came to get some stuff, Charl," he said. He was not unshaven, which was a pleasant surprise. However, I could tell he had returned to the habit of meat ingestion—his body reeked of animal fat (I maintain a fine-tuned sense of smell).

"Sure," I said.

"I don't want a scene," he said.

It sounded like some cliché from a hack film starring Sandra Bullock. It was disappointing.

"No," I simply said.

He stepped inside.

"What the hell?"

He was referring to the fact that by this point in the downward slope of our relationship I had painters glaze the entirety of my 3,623.25 square feet above in turquoise. My mentor said cool. Fish-bowl-esque colors would soothe me.

"I feel like some kind of sea cucumber, Charl."

"Well, good. That's the general idea. Or part of it. Why don't you come back? This is soothing, isn't it?"

He blew his nose into his sleeve; he knows how I find this to be counter-productive to his much-depleted energies.

"It's a bit too weird here for me," he said. "I just came to get some clothes. I'm tired of wearing the same shirt."

"Be my guest," I said. "Can I make you a bean sprout and edamame wrap? It's the twenty-fifth."

"See," he said, walking away. "That's exactly what I mean. I don't believe in that, in any of that."

I told him there was nothing to believe; uber-organic, numerological gustatory practices have been proven worldwide to promote energy construction. To wit, the article in *Sea Kelp* last month.

I still, sadly, associate the Tuvan throat music with Edward's final steps away from the love that once was ours. Long marriages, I assume, must find conclusion in one way or another. My mentor was the one who convinced me of this. I told her that eleven point two four months is not a particularly long stretch, but my mentor made the excellent point that this is only in Earth time. In the inner landscape where we all actually reside, our love lasted for eons. I mentioned to her the insight that Edward and I only had the rare occasion to share the intimacy that is the exchange of holy matrimonial fluids, but my wise mentor said this is no matter.

"The thrust of your love," she said, "is eternal, not merely physical."

At any rate I have chosen respite in the form of pillows. My mentor said pillows would help defuse the emotional violence of Ed's departure. I journeyed to one of our local home and bath retailers and pursued this line of thinking to the tune of twenty-nine pillows. Now I live within a soft fish tank, Ed says.

The use of the present tense is purposeful. I am still in active touch with my husband. The denouement here is that I still conduct healing upon him in the form of remote reiki, whether he shares this knowledge or not. He did mention to me not to "talk about that shit no more." At least he does refrain from clearing his nasal passages into his clothing in my presence.

I have subsequently found a wondrous new soul mate from the bus of soul mates which is our spherical orb. She emerged from the doors of the bus with an energy that bespoke of her royalty and divine spirit. Her name is Thistle Bud Chillington. Our union is purely nonsexual, and will remain so—as I physically lean towards the pull of the protuberances of men—but she has embraced reiki remote and otherwise with open wings. She adores the cool rapture of my azure walls and the pillows which I have towered hither and thither to suit my own healing purposes.

We drink tea together with vast abandon. My heart swells in the whirlpools of chai.

As it turns out I am now her mentor an am in the process of instructing her in the process and methodology of reiki remote and otherwise. The future is a vast plain on the bottom of the endless sea that is my voyage. And on this sea my healing is ceaseless.

# Norman Lock

## FROM *Pieces For Small Orchestra*

### 30.

He sets his theodolite on the bar glyphed by beer-glass bottoms; rubbled with cocktail napkins, tiny plastic swords, and peanut shells; anchored by elbows. It is polished brass and handsome—this instrument by which he measures two-dimensional space quaintly Euclidean now that an invisible lion in our midst has vanished into a parallel universe impossible, for us, to describe. "I am a Land Surveyor," he replies in answer to the Prime Minister's question. "But we have no need of surveying, sir!" the P.M. asserts with a belligerence, due, in part, to absinthe (which is not forbidden us) and ministerial habit. "This is a hotel!" he continues in this strain. "To take measurements, such as are within your ken, would be superfluous in light of this—" He indicates with an elegant hand the finished space around us. "Nothing here is provisional or conditional; everything is fixed, immutable, and—another, Bartender, if you please." He moves his empty glass an inch-and-one-half toward the absinthe bottle. "But I was summoned!" the Surveyor protests, much put out. "By whom?" "By me." The Physicist leans his lean length into the conversation to explain: "I wish to prove to my detractors that our hotel is swinging in and out of a visible dimension, according to String Theory's axioms as I have adapted them to suit the singularity of our existence, which is simultaneously imaginary and real." "O, so the Surveyor will play a role in another of the Physicist's thought experiments!" we moan, having been terrified by the last involving not one but three lions! "How do you propose to prove such a postulate?" the Prime Minister, whose head is 'big' at the moment from the dangerous intoxicant, demands. "The Surveyor will measure a room to determine whether or not it shrinks or expands, as I predict it must." The Surveyor requests a beer. "Put it on my tab," says the Plumber, who feels collegially toward this fellow of the building trades. The Surveyor quaffs and smiles at the lace of foam inside his empty glass. Not to be outdone by a Plumber, the General calls for drinks all round. The Physicist continues to elaborate: "I conjecture that the hotel is—in its essence—a vibration induced by our desire. It will shrink as the waveform flattens. At the point of climax, we will disappear. In other words, we are invisible to the outside world in proportion to our wish to be so." That night, the Surveyor measures the hotel lounge, where a row of barely dressed girls dance the hoochy-coochy. "What are your findings?" the Physicist inquires at the end of the floorshow. "The line of chorus girls is shorter," the Surveyor states with aplomb. The Physicist is elated, as are we. "Hooray! Let us now retire to our beds and dream, each in his own way and according to his disposition, a world cordial to moonlight serenades, poetry, and love."

### 40.

What excitement! The Director, who arrived "like a god" one afternoon on a piece of stage machinery lowered from the roof, will reenact Ben-Hur. The Palatine Hill, where Romulus and his brother Remus were mothered by a wolf, is nearly finished. Below it, remarkable reproductions of Roman barges ply a model Tyrrhenian Sea. "The Decorator has outdone himself!" the Soubrette praises. "Yes," the Prime Minister agrees, "his Circus Maximus is a masterpiece." We tremble to hear the pawing of Arabian steeds. Foaled by nightmares, they are confined in a corral warranted to withstand earthquakes and their aftershocks of 7 on the Richter Scale. Inspired by their terrible neighing, the Chanteuse trills a Cantata for Equus. "And who," the General asks, "is to be Ben-Hur, the Hebrew charioteer?" The Prime Minister, whose judgment is unclouded by sentiment or graft, nominates the Plumber. Indignant, the General rings his cavalry spur against a fluted column. "Only hands used to monkey-wrenches are strong enough to hold the reins." Blustering, the General reminds us of his equestrian exploits on a hill in Cuba. "That was long ago!" the PM snaps, and we detect a note of malice glittering like a scimitar's sharpened edge. "Pish!" the old man sputters. "You shall play the part of Tiberius," the P. M. says, relenting. "The Roman Emperor?" "None other." How the General beams to have been accorded such an honor! "But I don't have a toga, or is that just for Greeks?" "There are hampers brimming with costumes from every period," says the Soubrette, who, for the nonce, is acting as the drama's Costumier. The General claps his hands and hurries off. "Who is to play Messalah and race his chariot against Ben-Hur's?" inquires the Historian in his capacity as technical adviser. "Norman." "No, I'm out of shape and easily tired!" I protest. "Hmmmm. What about the Carpenter?" the Decorator suggests. "He's brawny and unafraid of horses." "An excellent choice!" approves the PM The day arrives for which we have been waiting. The circus seats are crowded. The guests, attired picturesquely like first century Anno Domini Roman citizens, are eating hotdogs and drinking beer in paper cups. Despite a reputation as a tyrant on the set, the Director is unable to forbid anachronisms such as these, as well as a musical score played on modern instruments. Anticipating blood and mayhem, the hotel Physician is ecstatic. There is little to occupy a man of his profession when sickness and injury are virtually extinct. I sit by the Shepherdess, who looks suitable to any age, and admire the Roman maidens in their décolletage, while on the Tiber galley slaves contend with currents flustered by a wind-machine. Now, a fanfare blares in the cyclorama's cloudless sky. The Emperor drops a handkerchief and, when it has finished fluttering to the rutted track, the race begins. Four chariots leap and rattle down the lanes, pulled by horses whipped to fury. Obedient to the oval, the chariots orbit until there are only two that interest us: Ben-Hur's and his former friend Messalah's, whose wheels are equipped with turning blades! He hopes, with them, to dismantle the Jew's, which lacks accessories. In spite of them, Ben-Hur's enemy tumbles from his chariot. The Physician rushes to his mangled side, a smile on his lips; and with instruments once used by his father to tend to duelers, practises his healing art on the Roman, who, notwithstanding, dies. A shadow, scarcely noticed, has been crawling across the churned and bloody sand. Aware of it at last, I think it cast by a vulture or other bird of death—a finale provided by the Director for his spectacle. But looking up, I see my tightrope-walking wife, passing loftily over Circus Maximus. She ignores the kiss I throw her, doubtlessly annoyed by the Shepherdess at my side. "She means nothing!" I shout. But the high-wire artiste, who has forsworn the ground, does not stop to answer.

# Carol Novack

## Dance, Baby, Dance!

### 1. Prom Queen

Baby pink clouds chased the little sailboat till it slipped off the edge of the sea. From afar, I heard the boys zithering in the wind. When I turned to bite your ear lobe, the alarming scent of prom orchids assaulted me. You offered them, but I had no gown and I was much too old for that sort of thing. So I wept. To comfort me, you stroked my tender bellybutton, sore from a storm of births. We returned to the shore, passing the abandoned tennis court where you'd kidnapped my virginity and throttled me twenty-love. The sailboat was landing with its cargo of boys. Now men, they were hung like dung beetles coughing in the breeze. The biggest and fattest one approached. "Dance, baby, dance," he screamed, wrapping his blubbery legs about my nether regions. Brushing him off, I told him, "I don't care for marshmallows," then turned to find you'd disappeared off the edge of memory.

### 2. Football Hero

He persists in returning to the field. Ever since the story of his third marriage ended, he's been looking for the Prom Queen. When he approaches the players, the coaches call him predator, old fag. The mothers will throw their lawyers at him, thinking unspeakable things. He only wants to dance and play in the Queen's white cotton panties. She demanded he eat no more than one pomegranate seed a day till his helmet became a tourniquet and his shoulder pads gave him backaches. All those years, the work didn't work; in the end he couldn't catch the tires rolling along assembly lines, tires smelling of road-kill, his third wife's suffocating perfume. On his custody day, he leads his daughter to the arena of the football heroes. When she rolls her eyes, oh daddy, he takes her to the shore, watches ocean liners evaporate in fog while she hugs her cell phone to her ear, speaks awesome whatever to her tennis star. There is nothing between the lapsed football hero and the sea, nothing to keep him from searching for his Queen under her waves.

### 3. Ebbing

There are no boats riding the fog in a dead wind. Turning toward you, I notice thin strands of fresh blond hair in your teeth. Still asleep, with lids fluttering, you are once again dreaming of the Prom Queen. You with your whale belly float while I fill your breakfast bowl with fruits from the garden and hide nuts and bitter seeds inside of them, hoping your teeth will fall out. Then you will abandon the tennis courts and forget her. The Queen is now wizened and waned with dusty silver mouse hair and breasts like racquets. Though there are times I don't want to catch you, there is no one else and you know I'm afraid of water.

# Tim Poland

## Brazilian Mahogany

Inside the house, we didn't even hear it. From this distance, you would think such a thing would make a sound capable of cutting through anything—squealing rubber, torn steel, shattered glass, ripped tree limbs, gnashing gears, that baby wailing. But with Miles Davis's "Kind of Blue" on the stereo and the house bustling with people from the home tour and the doors and double-paned windows closed for the air conditioning, honestly, we didn't hear a thing. As it was, one of the tour people on the deck thrust her head inside the door and shouted, "My cell phone's dead. Someone call 911 or something." Then I saw it, we all saw it. A small SUV, Subaru Forester, had leapt a guardrail on the Clara Barton Parkway adjacent to and above the copse of trees behind the house, torn through the branches of one of the larger elms, and landed upside down, the front end and windshield mashed into the ground, the rest of the vehicle relatively intact but for the torn and bent side panels.

Everyone approached the car cautiously, as if the crash were still in progress, as if the car might yet explode, fearful of first-hand witness of the carnage that must lie within. If the car hadn't flipped and landed upside down, perhaps some sort of rapid rescue could have been accomplished by those of us there—perhaps a clear-thinking, composed, temporary hero might have issued from the group of home tour visitors, freed the passengers quickly, and saved the home tour from complete disaster, in fact providing an additional layer of excitement and entertainment that might only show the house off better. But mashed down as it was on the front end, we couldn't gain access, couldn't even see inside the vehicle. Not clearly. Even that might have been something we could have borne until the EMS crew arrived. What could one do, really, in such a situation? We weren't equipped for it. This was work for trucks with winches, ambulances, police officers, and professionals in dark blue jumpsuits armed with sophisticated medical kits. The driver was probably dead, probably drunk and responsible for his fate anyway. It would have been reasonable to arrive at such an assumption and just wait for the trucks and ambulances and professionals that would, after all, be dutifully summoned, to arrive—if not for the sound of crying within the wreckage. Not the whimpering of an adult in pain but the full-throated wailing of an infant. More than anyone could be expected to bear. Certainly more than she could bear, in the end, given the circumstances.

We'd been in the house a year at that point, with the remodeling work proceeding non-stop, for the most part. The final touches had just been completed—the floor of Brazilian mahogany newly-laid in the kitchen/breakfast area, the Black Galaxy Indian granite counter tops with ogee edges in place, the Sub-Zero PRO 48 refrigerator with glass panel door and the six-burner Wolf gas range with dual convection ovens installed. In truth, the floors are andiroba, but it's commonly called Brazilian mahogany, which pleases me since the word connotes more effectively the richness of the wood. Including our house on the Bethesda Summer Tour of Homes was a way to show off the accomplishment. A commemoration. From this place we would begin again. Leave history behind. Forget everything that ever happened before we met at the retreat in Cabo—my ex-wife and both daughters refusing to even look at me, to be in the same room with me, let alone speak to me—her first husband and five-year-old son threaded through the axles of a semi on I-95. Here, looking over the newly-finished deck, into the copse of trees enclosing the back of the lot, protecting us from the parkway, listening to Miles Davis, here we could hold onto a cup of freshly-ground coffee or a glass of Bordeaux, could hold onto each other, could use words like copse, and be released from our pasts. Just the two of us, in the present. In this present, so carefully constructed. Everything clean and new and in place.

I had called 911 on the land line while everyone else, including her, deserted the house to join the others around the wreckage. By the time I arrived outside one of the women from the home tour group was on her knees, whimpering, clawing at the rear passenger side door. "Oh god, it's a baby. Get it out. It's just a baby. Oh, god." Her fingers were already torn and bleeding, desperate to get a grip on the door, which was caved in from the crash and wedged shut. We tried to pull her away, but she shrugged us off, frantic in her assault on the closed door. The strength in her arms and shoulders startled me. The wailing of the infant was overwhelming, just inches from us, but unreachable, unstoppable. We could barely see through the web of fissures in the cracked window, just enough to make out the red-faced baby, strapped in its safety seat, upside down and howling. We could barely get a view of the driver, just that she was a woman, the mother, we assumed, and that she was still, twisted, and bloodied.

We continued to try to calm the woman, assure her that the rescue squad would arrive soon, and she continued to refuse our entreaties. One of the men in the group of home tour visitors came running from his car, a tire iron in hand to pry at the jammed door when the first ambulance arrived, other sirens not far behind. Professionals had arrived to take control of the situation, just as they were supposed to do. I turned my eyes to the ambulance as it lurched into the drive and saw her, my second wife, at the back of the crowd of home tour visitors around the Subaru. She stood still as a tree, rooted, her arms folded tightly onto her stomach, as if screwed down, her lips pressed so firmly together they seemed but one lip. Her gaze was locked on the wrecked car, fixed, stony as a slab of granite.

If only the guard rail had kept that car up on the parkway as intended, if only the car hadn't landed upside down, if only the mother hadn't been mashed, snapping her neck, if only the EMS squad hadn't had to treat that home tour woman's mangled fingers and sedate her—if only that baby hadn't been strapped in there crying. If only it had happened some other day, any other day, not during the tour of homes, after all the renovations, then we'd be fine, safe and free, and she would be what I wanted her to be and wouldn't be lying in bed all day, every day, her fingers picking at the embroidery on the Italian duvet cover, staring at the ceiling, indifferent to me, to our new lives free of history.

In the late afternoon light, the reflection of the Sub-Zero PRO 48 on the polished Brazilian mahogany floor is dazzling.

# Tiffany Promise

## Every Hollow Thing

"Have you seen this house? It's so purple," I hear—ears barely straining through quadruple-paned windows that are not paned enough. I am curled on the slate couch, with the fabric somewhere between supple and straw. I can't remember if people are safe anymore. Even the voices that seem honeyed might have razor edges. I hate that anyone can see my house, that it can't just be invisible like me.

There are some cats in this room with me. They lick and purr and knead. I feed them on schedule, though the hours between feedings sometimes feel longer than others. We take up this space together, take in this oxygen, give it little back in return: piss, shit, sloughed skin cells, abandoned hair and fur. Every now and again we lose fingernails and claws, whiskers, eyelashes, blood. We mark this space as our own—hoping that no one will wish to trespass.

There are things worse than floods to contend with, and we used to think floods were the worst. We have marched two by two onto four by fours. Planked and heavy, full of soak. But the waters always recede and we come back home, or make home wherever we need to make it.

"Your non-fiction is my fiction," the voice says, garbled under too much red wine. I wonder if her throat were slashed if merlot would pour out instead of blood.

Sometimes there is nowhere to go but inside. Inside is often the best place. There are no actual sunsets here, or beaches, cafes, flea markets, parks, Eiffel towers. But that's okay. We've got irises and organs and indefinite night.

"Have you eaten yet?" she asks.

"A nibble of brioche, some dried apricots, and salted pecans. I shared a glass of milk with Camille. There were also a few pretzels thrown in, but I'm not sure if that was today or yesterday—the days leak together like watercolors: yesterday a sailboat, today an English countryside."

Last week there was an apple, I know that for sure, because I remember the shine on its bright skin. It didn't look real—like plastic or paint or some toxic something or other that would have been deadly to my fragile hollows. I peeled it off carefully with a knife. The insides were soft and sweet and trustworthy. Usually, poison sticks to the exterior, glazing over everything with its too-bright doom. Unluckily for Snow White, her apple was sullied through and through. But there was no old hag delivering my apple, just a grocery delivery boy with a scruffy beard and nose ring.

There are soft rasps that have been coming out of the front hall closet. I don't mind. I trust ghosts more than I do people. The cats sometimes get startled and their tails flick in mischievousness. They can see more than me: flashes of light particles in air that might be otherworldly. I can smell as much as them: the rotting of our wooden beams being snacked on by too many beetles. We are scared of the floors falling out from under us, but we know that there is ground down there that can hold us steady. It is the walls falling down that really worry—daggering eyes live on the other side of our edges. We have been doing a lot of layering lately, in case the bugs win and we need immediate protection. I ordered 55 black cashmere sweaters from Neiman's. They have pearl buttons and black, silk ribboning. They arrived in loads of cardboard and tissue. Even though I ordered extra smalls for the cats, they still drag, collecting dust on the hems.

"Your present is my past," the voice throbs. She undulates slowly, bobbing from one foot to the other, a tiny almost-earthquake passes through my curtains.

"My present is my present is my present," I whisper heatedly, hoping that maybe I can trip her with my vehemence. If she fell though, it would take a while for her to get up. Under all that alcohol, her already-weighted body is weighted. She is massive, like a boulder. I would rather her not settle in front of my window for good, eking out opinions like a lobotomized poet, growing mushrooms and daisies for the passerby.

I take my vitamins, check to make sure that the locks are secure, have a cup of enzyme tea, and share some yoghurt with Camille. I like a drop of agave; she likes plain. We refasten any buttons that have come loose, and we sit in front of the fireplace like spinsters without any yarn. We are wearing every last inch of wool in the house and it is as delicate as cobwebs, but warmer still. We listen for the hall closet echoes, and we say a quick prayer against collapse.

"Shit, I lost you," comes a guttural mumble. I peek out, and see her looking down, agitatedly pulsating the screen in her hand, turning her face a bitter shade of goblin.

"You never had me!" I bellow, feeling each word course through me like a steam engine. I am alive with abhorrence. Camille curves her spine like a Halloween cat, and flicks her tail at my reddened face. I relax as I hear the feet begin to re-slug themselves up the hill, carrying the interloper away.

I sometimes wish for a better protector: cats and ghosts don't have too much muscle between them. But, when my heart beats a sonnet, I am reminded of my own muscle. Invisibility doesn't preclude anatomy. My myocardium divides the inside and the outside, and beats with the ferocity of a thunderstorm. Every hollow thing yearns to be filled with something, whether it be blood, food, love, furniture, phantoms. You never had me. But I wish that you had.

# Carole Rosenthal

## Fusion

The couple upstairs is fighting again. Or moving furniture.

"No they're not! They're fucking." Arnie pulls his lower lip up to hide a grin, and yanks me down onto the bed next to him, grabbing at my toes and trapping them between his legs. Just correcting me gives him an erection. You can imagine how much he gets off on his students when he's teaching. In fact, we met when he was the teaching assistant in my advanced zoology lab. Years ago.

Not five minutes has passed since he told me he was too tired to even talk. He'd been working on laboratory slides all day, peering into microscopes, couldn't I understand how exhausted he was, why was I trying to have a serious discussion with him? He covers my face with slippery snail tracks of affection.

"How do you know what they're doing?" I ask. "They're so noisy."

"Would they move furniture every single night? You think we have interior decorators in this tenement?"

Later, when I'm in the bathtub, a watery trickle of blood falls through a crack in the ceiling onto the white tile floor. "Help!" I yell to Arnie. "Call the police, they're killing each other!"

"Rust," Arnie says, slipping his fingers into the redness and sniffing. His voice is crisp and factual as he bends over, the Voice of Science. But my panic excites him.

He carries me into the bedroom on his back, fireman-style—though I'd like it better frontways (like Rhett took Scarlett, like King Kong took Fay Wray)—and he levers me off his shoulder like a backpack. I fall spread-eagled below him and pretend to be asleep.

"Do you like what I'm doing?" he asks me, his head bobbing upward from my belly and pushing next to my cheek on the pillow. "You should tell me, I want to know."

"Yes," I nod against him. His skin feels loose, a size too large. It scares me. Since his thirty-fourth birthday last month I worry a lot about his mortality, about how fragile our connection is, about blue veins forking helplessly beneath his surface and lying thick and passive above his thighs and along his cock, throbbing susceptibly in his temples. What if he leaves me? What if has a heart attack?

I've got to stop feeding him salted soft-boiled eggs for breakfast. All that cholesterol. I lick the shallow cavity between his ribs and worry.

"What're you thinking?" He turns off the light, stretching, then smiling and issuing instructions. "Why don't you talk to me? Talk dirty." He tells me what he wants to hear and how to say it. "Use your legs like calipers," he urges. "But gently, gently."

His mouth comes over my face like a hollow tube. A laboratory siphon. My head begins to spin, separating my thoughts from the feelings. My eyes shut.

I'm fixating on light splotches behind the lids, the colors are shooting into my head and I feel myself being rolled over and pressed down beneath his moist body weight. He checks to make sure that my diaphragm is inserted correctly and then begins kneading me like yeasted dough beneath his fingers, pulling at my flesh. I am growing bigger, budding, rising. Growing right up against the corners of the room.

*

"I want a baby," I tell him, but he's not listening. He's sleeping. I'm sitting in our apartment four flights up with my nose pressed against the cold morning windowpane, the sunlight reflecting into my eyes from the steel building across the way.

I don't like being alone in the morning. It makes me nervous.

"Wake up, Arnie, it's already half-past ten. Get up, I want to talk with you."

Even though we tangled close for sleep last night, we weren't touching this morning. He sleeps with one arm cupped, protected, between his thighs. There's something inviolable about him even in sleep. The curl of his lip, or maybe the color of his hair which is filing cabinet gray against the sheets.

When he opens his eyes he can't understand why I'm bothering him, why not let him curl into his Sunday morning dreams like other members of the zoology department.

"Fill in crosswords. Amuse yourself with funnies from the Daily News, Becky!"

And: "This is my weekend, Becky. I let you do what you want, why can't you leave me alone?"

"I want a baby," I say. "I'm almost thirty years old. We're both getting older."

He simulates a snore.

We've had this discussion—a fight really—a hundred times before, a billion times it feels like. What does a baby represent, he wants to know, talking about finances and responsibility. I talk about love. The form is so ritualized I hardly know much I mean what I claim.

"You're not even paying attention to me," I say. And finally, I begin to cry. His jaw, marked with shadows, juts out.

I picture my ovaries: a tin of open caviar that has been sitting too long in the refrigerator, the little black eggs getting harder and tinier, until finally they have to be scraped with a spoon and flushed away.

Abruptly he sits up, not looking at me. "Oh, for the love of it, stop feeling sorry for yourself! I don't know why we have to plan the future of mankind before we even get breakfast."

"You used to say we'd decide as soon as they put you in charge of the laboratory."

"Sure, he says, folding his arms across his chest and pulling into himself, his knees close together, so tight the air around him is vacuum suction. "Do you really want a baby?"

"Really, yes."

"And not a new job? Or plants, or tropical fish? How about a Burmese kitten, or a border collie pup, you'd probably like that." Then: "Just teasing. You know."

"I want you to take me seriously. I want a permanent connection between us, something created by—"

"Crap! Do you think you can send a kid across the street to pick up a carton of milk for his breakfast? How'll we pay for it, who's going to change the diapers and get up in the night?

"I've got an 8 a.m. lecture to give, so? Try worrying about a kid instead of about me or yourself and it's going to be twice as painful, you'll see. We're young. That's a lot of responsibility you're talking so cheap."

"But I'm prepared. We weren't a few years ago, but I am now. Besides," I touch the tip of my nose with my finger, a sign of honesty from my childhood, "we said when we were first together that we could have a baby. You promised!"

His lips pull in against his teeth, tight, flattened until puffs of laughter push them out. He shakes his head, rocking forward, and squints like he's sizing me up. "You," he says. "You want to be a child, not to have a child."

Tilting his head, as if he's taking me in. Dissecting me with his distance, peeling my skin back, cutting me down smaller and smaller until I almost disappear. Turning, bracing myself on the glass, I stare into the sun above the roofs. Maybe I don't love him after all.

Back in the room, I see a tall silhouette edging off the bed--he could be anybody, no one special—he is all angles reaching a gray hand out to me. "Don't be upset. Do you really want a baby? I'm only kidding, we can talk about it...."

He begins stroking me with dark fingers, there are sunbursts in my eyes, scintillae disintegrate from him as he leads me to the bed. My breath is methane gas around him, my body, cooling, a foreign planet. Unreceptive. How does he survive. There is no life here. Slowly, I grow swampy.

"We could make a beautiful baby," he says, teasing, taking little sucks out of the back of my neck, sponging the light on my cheeks with his brow. "Do you really think I'm serious. I've just been waiting for the right time."

"You're making fun of me."

"No," he promises, spreading his legs against the sheet and lowering himself slowly, his vertebrae uncurling, serpentine from Yoga exercises each morning. "I really mean it." He's not smiling, he's almost crooning. "If you want to have a baby, we can have one but you have to be the adult who takes care of it during the day."

I think it over while white stars shoot around the room and bust open, while he pulls me down onto his body and prongs his penis into my mouth.

"Do I have to take care of it all by myself?"

"I'm in the laboratory, working all day." He strokes my face with his penis. There are oceans on my body, crusts form, resistant but not unyielding. "You have to watch the baby during the daytime."

"What if I break it?"

"I'll make you a new one. And if you want to give it away, we'll sell it. Do you like that idea?" But his voice suddenly stops coaxing, his Science voice again. "As a matter of fact, Becky, that's not so absurd. It's extremely difficult to produce good white babies anymore, do you realize we could probably trade a child—a good-looking high-IQ child—for seventy-five or a hundred thousand, maybe more." The slow-voiced again, amused, steering me to his prick. "So come on, just pretend it's an ice cream cone and you can have whatever you want."

"A baby!" I cry.

"Yes, baby," he says as my lips fit over him and he begins to growl back in his throat like a canine, his eyes uplifted and rolling. "Oh, come on, baby, that's the way I like it, yes, give me some tongue."

His finger is sticking into me, splitting me in two. This is the beginning of mitosis, cell division; he saws me with his finger. I don't need his sperm to come into me, to fertilize me,

I am simpler than that. I don't need him at all, I am an amoeba, I split and have my children, I fuse and have my sex. My own child, my own parent, creating myself endlessly.

"Baby," he is arching backwards, he looks as if he is creating the universe, crowding inside me, thronging life into my mouth, proud. I swallow. I am all hollow stomach.

I open my mouth, breathe deeply, fill myself with air. Blow up, evolve. Damn him, I am not so simple as that! Not just an amoeba, a harmless blob. Does he think I'll take any shape I'm pushed into? Let him leave me if he wants!

No, I am bright blue, purple, phylum coelenterata, traveling up the evolutionary ladder. I'm a Portuguese man o'war leaking enzymes, devouring, eddying in the air inside our bedroom. Alternating: sexual, asexual.

"Did you mean that about the baby?" I say. "Why did you come in my mouth, then?"

I'm getting bigger, thrusting outward, aggressive, pink-crested with anger, caught up by a riptide that catches the long knots trailing from me, poisonous, stinging nematocysts. They paralyze. He doesn't move.

"You just said that to get me to do what you wanted, didn't you?"

But he flexes himself away from me onto the mattress, then pushes me down, spreading his arms wide and lying on top of me full weight.

"Roll over," he says.

"You're squishing me," I call, but it's as if he's buoyed up on my body and hardly hears me; he begins pressing the air out of me, pumping me down. Flattening, I'm diminishing. And then, almost gratefully, I realize that I'm a planarian, flat and cute with crossed over eyespots. I can barely feel anything, my nerves are fused into a small knot, primitive ganglia.

Then, as he enters me, finding somewhere an opening, I begin to roll into shape, a round worm, a nematode, I'm churning the earth, writhing up, up, taking different forms. And now I am changing again, hanging onto him with pincers, then scuttling, silent, away from him as he rearranges himself above. To watch him I turn my skinny stalk eyes, phylum arthropoda, a lobster, curling my body upwards as the tension mounts. He mounts me, I'm almost a chordate I can feel my bones, sharp, sticking into my flesh, a sun-mottled carp.

"Are you wearing your diaphragm?" he asks. Usually he checks me with his finger before we start. He doesn't trust me. But this time when I nod my head he doesn't stop to find out that I am lying about the rubber stopper, the cap, the plug in the earth. His body presses into me. I hear the sound of wings, a flapping, class aves. Almost human …

"I'm coming," he says, releasing his life into me, premature amphibians, tadpoles, thousands, millions of baby froggies, black and swimming, no legs—like the ones he poured down the sink of his laboratory—into me. They're swimming like crazy, flagellating, they want to live, they want to join with the caviar eggs inside me. I'm not going to stop them.

"I'm coming," he whispers into my ear, beginning to moan, pressing against me, his teeth against my mammalian nipple, a man thrusting his life and history into my core.

"Oh, baby, I'm coming.…"

Strange. Even unhappy. I don't know how to stop him.

# Max Ruback

## Sand

Somalia, Africa.

A desert, waves of sand. Mild winds made a rain of the baking sand, which came at you from the ground up, pricking your skin, leaving dots of red burns. Soldiers stuffed cotton in their ears and nostrils. Sand got in everything: eyes, food, equipment. It kept helicopters grounded, machine-gun triggers stuck, powdered eggs gritty. Sand mites and cameramen everywhere. Even the soldiers had camcorders. Whatever it was they were doing here, it didn't much feel like war, or a peace-keeping mission, or whatever it was supposed to be. It sort of had the feeling of a home movie.

One night, he dreamt he was blind and walking through a sandstorm, sand filling his mouth and going down his throat. He struggled to breathe, began to choke, which was the point when he woke up, his heart beating fast, looking around the darkened tent, the taste of sand in his mouth. He had only been asleep for twenty minutes and was dying of thirst.

You couldn't drink enough water. You walked around bloated. You were always thirsty. Always pissing.

In an early letter home, he wrote how beautiful the desert sky was at dusk, how he was friendly with a group of Somalian kids that were teaching him their language. In a way, to actually see the starving people made him appreciate the life he had back home in the United States. He felt he was maturing, and that he had been doing a lot of thinking, and he regretted many things. But he didn't include that. Or make mention of the sand, or the scorpions, or the feeling of being homesick, or the legless boy who was pulled around on a piece of cardboard by his mother.

He was trying to be a man, and men didn't complain about such things to their mothers.

One day, he watched a bunch of Somalian kids literally fight over a pack of M&M's. They did not want to share.

It started to wear on him—the starvation and the heat and the sand and the smell of garbage decomposing and burning, the sporadic gunfire. He stopped looking in his shoes for scorpions. Whatever happened, happened. Poker helped. He played a lot of poker. The stakes got higher the longer they were there: from packs of Kool-Aid to cigarettes to money to favors. Soldiers got a kick when a fellow soldier lost his shirt. He wasn't a very good bluffer, but he just liked taking part in the games. A good game of poker could take your mind off anything, each and every soldier talking about something, anything, agreeing for the sake of agreeing and disagreeing for the sake of talking, laughing for its own sake.

There were good times. For instance, one day as the sun was setting, a group of soldiers got a football game together and played two-hand touch until it was dark. Then they lit flares, stuck them in the ground and played a little longer. They did that for a couple of days, but then the football got stolen. Something was always being stolen. You couldn't trust the Somalians, and you couldn't trust other soldiers. The next day, they found another platoon with a football that resembled the one they had lost. A fight almost broke out between two soldiers who were looking to start something, but they were pulled apart and told to calm down. Instead, the platoons played a game, winner take ball. They planted machine guns in the ground to mark the endzones. The game started in the fashion of two-hand touch, but after about ten minutes they changed to playing tackle. He got in the game after another soldier pulled his hamstring. He caught a pass and got hit hard, got sand in his mouth. He called the soldier an asshole.

"You say something?" the soldier said.

He walked back to the huddle.

"You say something?" The soldier got in his face. "You afraid to say something now, little man? I am the meanest motherfucker you will ever know. You don't want to get in the way of my shit. I will tear your head off and shit down your neck." He beat on his chest like a gorilla. The soldiers were always trying to act crazy or deranged in some way, looking for a reputation, a nickname. He tried to ignore him.

Soldiers sat on a tank and watched, laughing, egging the violence on. A group of Somalians became spectators, knowing this wasn't the kind of game they were wanted in. So they chose sides, clapping their hands when someone scored. Somalian women poured water from plastic jugs over the bodies of the soldiers to get the sand out of their cuts and replenish their fluids. Shouting kids tackled one another. Heatstroke caused players to quit, but the game continued. Tired players were replaced by soldiers wanting to get some aggression out. Nobody kept score. Jets screamed across the sky. Fights broke out, but the game kept going. A soldier suffered a compound fracture, but the game did not end there, even though it was a blowout. It wasn't about the score anymore. One soldier lost some teeth. A few got bloody noses.

Just before sunset, a wind blew wisps of sand into the air. A Somalian woman, tucking her baby's face under her breast, began singing. The others followed. They gathered their children, and within minutes a sandstorm came, and the soldiers headed back to camp. The women led, their children singing along.

# Thaddeus Rutkowski

## City Visit

When I first saw the city, I thought it was filled with hospitals. The buildings visible through our family car's windshield were rectangular, with rows of identical windows. To me, the buildings looked like the county hospital where my mother worked. "What kind of hospitals are those?" I asked my father.

He turned from the steering wheel and said, "They're apartments."

Next to him, my mother made no comment. In the back seat, my brother and sister showed no interest in the structures. Suddenly, the buildings vanished as we entered a tunnel and my father turned on the car's headlights.

In the city, the streets were strewn with newspapers. The wheels of our car kicked up the sheets of newsprint as we rolled.

"We never liked the city when we lived here," my father said. "That was years ago, before you kids were born."

"I could walk to my training program at a hospital," my mother said.

"They found the head of a person in one trash can," my father said, "and the body in another, right outside our apartment building."

\*

We went through a metal door to get into the building where my father's friend Steve lived. We took a lever-operated elevator, then walked through a sliding metal door into a loft. The space had only a couple of pieces of furniture: a foldout couch, a glass coffee table and a bed. Clotheslines were strung from wall to wall. Most of the space was taken up by worktables with silkscreen presses on them.

In the bathroom, the toilet bowl was cracked, and the water tank was near the ceiling. "Don't worry about it," Steve said. "It works like this." He made a sound in his throat of gurgling, rushing water, then of banging metal. "Just pull the handle."

"Whatever you do," my father said, "don't open the front door for anyone."

Later, there was a knock at the door. Without asking who it was, my mother unlatched the lock and slid the metal bar open. A young woman was standing outside. She had straight brown hair pulled into a ponytail and appeared harmless. She turned out to be Steve's girlfriend, Pat.

\*

In the loft, there wasn't much for me and my siblings to do except play with the resident cat. We threw a string out a window and let it dangle down to the tar-covered rooftop below. A cat prowled on the lower surface. When it saw our string, it batted at the moving strand.

When my turn came, I cast the string out the window. I worked the line from side to side, jiggling it, until I felt resistance. "I got a strike!" I announced.

I "landed" the cat as I wound the string back up through the window. The cat jumped onto the sill and chased the end of the string into the room. "Got him!" I said.

"You're a good cat-fisherman," my brother said.

\*

In the evening, Steve showed a black-and-white film. "It's called *The Bird*," he said. "It's been screened in art museums and galleries all over the world. These actors are stars in foreign cities."

In the movie, Pat was wearing a tutu, tights and ballet slippers. She ran over rooftops as a man in a bear suit chased her. A man in a clown suit chased the man in a bear suit.

"Those are our neighbors," Steve said, referring to the men in costume, "They do it all—art, teaching, acting."

When the bear and the clown got tired of running, they left the picture. In the end, Pat was alone on a tarpaper rooftop, next to a water tank, dancing.

"Look at this," Steve said. He brought out an old issue of *Time* magazine and pointed at the cover. The layout showed a collection of posters under the headline "Happenings."

"See?" Steve added. "There it is!" We all looked closely and saw a postage-stamp flyer for *The Bird*.

"That's great," my father said, "but I don't make popular art; I make real art."

\*

At night, I slept on an air mattress on the floor, and the rest of my family slept on the foldout couch. My siblings were small, so there was room for all of them.

In the middle of the night, I saw Steve get up—no walls divided the space. Naked, he walked across the floor, under the clotheslines. Over his head, paper silkscreen prints hung from clothespins.

Once awake, I noticed that the air had gone out of my mattress, I was resting on the hard floor. I blew up the mattress, but I was too tired to inflate it the whole way. When morning came, I was again lying on the floor, with only a sheet of plastic between my body and the wood.

\*

During the day, my family visited the city's main zoo. We walked through an aviary and past many animals in cages, then stopped in front of a rock garden that held gorillas. "They're so handsome," my mother said.

I looked at the male gorillas' protruding brows, huge shoulders, short legs and long arms. Their hair was matted. To me, the creatures were ugly. When they looked at me, they seemed to know what I was thinking. They studied me with hatred.

"I want to take a picture," my mother said.

My father handed her a Brownie camera, and she held it in front of her waist so she could look through the viewfinder. She pressed the shutter button a couple of times.

"We didn't have gorillas where I grew up," she said. "We had pandas, in the bamboo forests, where tribes lived."

"Which tribes?" I asked.

"You'd call them aboriginal Chinese."

"We want to see the pandas!" my brother and sister said.

The zoo, as it turned out, had no pandas.

My sister picked up on a pop song she'd heard and sang it repeatedly for the rest of the day. She could carry a tune, but the sound of her voice hitting the same notes and phrasings soon became bothersome.

*

Back at Steve's place, my father looked into cabinets until he found some opened bottles of liquor. He drank what was left and returned the empties.

"A gorilla is not very smart," he said to my mother. "Why do you prefer a gorilla to me?"

"They are very handsome," my mother said.

"I don't need handsome," my father said, "and I don't need a family. That's my problem—a wife and kids. I'd be better off without you."

When Steve came home, he opened cabinet doors and asked, "What happened to my whiskey?"

"I drank it," my father said, "and now I'm going out to get more. I'm going to shake up this city."

At that moment, my father pitched forward. The bottom of his chin hit the edge of the glass coffee table. He twitched once or twice, then lay on the floor unconscious. A gash on his chin looked like a second mouth.

My mother took my father to a hospital emergency room. When they came back, my father was wearing a bandage. When Pat saw it, she asked, "What happened?"

"I cut myself shaving," my father said.

"The hospital was just like the one where I trained," my mother said.

\*

On the way home, my sister was still singing the pop song she'd heard. Because we were in a car, there was no way to avoid it.

My father was driving erratically. The bandage on his chin had been changed to a smaller one. Stitches were visible in his skin. At one point, I thought I saw a car coming the wrong way—toward us—on the interstate. I didn't know how it got into the wrong lane. Was it a police car, or a car with a drunk driver? I thought it might veer into our path, but it just passed us by.

\*

Later, when my parents got their photos developed, I looked through the stack until I found the shots of the gorillas. The look in their eyes was as baleful as ever. Still, I sorted through the prints and gave the ones of the giant males to my mother.

# Lynda Schor

## Failure of Vision

*Exercise*: The Sands of Time
*Intention*: To end a relationship
*Frequency*: Twice a day (early morning and twilight) for up to three minutes, for seven days

Close your eyes. Breathe in and out three times and see yourself walking along a beach holding hands with the one with whom you are ending the relationship. The two of you are dancing, skipping, cavorting along the beach. Then you drop hands, say good-bye, and retrace your steps backwards thoroughly erasing everything that you see before you. Finally you reach the shoreline. The waves wash away all the residue of the relationship. You then swim to the horizon, using a regular crawl stroke, seeing your arms, legs, and torso elongating. Meet the horizon and come back to shore using a backstroke, your arms stretched out far above your head, your legs stretched far in front of you, kicking. When you reach the shore, come out and let the sun dry you. Put on a clean robe or gown and return to your home. Then open your eyes.

… and find yourself surrounded by your dusty floor that was sanded not by the person you are trying to break from, but your former husband, who did a lousy job, leaving cracks and splinters, and applying a polyurethane that never completely dried. You are wearing one of his old huge t-shirts—the one with the photo of Kafka on it, who, with his pointy ears and intense eyes, looks like a bat. You can recall the last time you were at a beach but can't recall the last time you cavorted. Steve, the person you are visualizing ridding yourself of, is not someone who cavorts either. However, you can both swim. Even though it's only six a.m., you can hear your four-year-old, Ivan, beginning to pant in the next room. That means he's getting hungry. But you are sick to death of your routine, which is Ivan's lifeline. How on earth did you acquire a child who likes each moment of the day to be exactly the same, who will only eat the same foods prepared the same way at the same time? Instead of getting up to prepare Ivan's toast and peanut butter, you lie there, the slightly curved end of your spine pressing into the floorboards, the small of your back much higher off the floor than it should be, and you recall the last time you heard from Steve, which was three weeks ago. He takes you to the beach in his two-tone brown Chevrolet that has cardboard in the back right window. Your son Ivan is with his father (he goes with his father, not regularly, but only when his dad has a whim) but Steve's six-year-old, Nicholas, sits in the back seat of the car, not wearing his seatbelt. He's tall for his age, but, unlike his father, fine-boned. In fact, he looks nothing like Steve, who is tall and burly, dark-skinned, with dark hair and a long, equine face. Steve looks, in fact, like your father. Every time Steve looks at Nicholas, with his small round face, buttercup blond hair and small blue eyes, he recalls Nicholas' mother Bebe, who hates Steve, and, according to Steve, has good reason, which is probably what you like about him. Still, according to Steve, Bebe can be quite the bitch.

 Steve doesn't say much, but you're used to his silence and feel quite comfortable. Your father didn't talk much either, though you weren't comfortable with him—you always felt there was something you should say to keep him entertained—and it made you tense. But with Steve it doesn't matter if you say anything— you keep him entertained in bed. Your father was (I'll give him credit for this) immune to your teenaged attempts at seduction, preferring, incomprehensibly, your mother. Deborah Tannen writes that silence can be used as a weapon, frustrating efforts to communicate. You realize that your father used his silence that way with your mother, but not with you. Steve is in a bad mood. He seems angry at Nicholas, but he might really be angry at Bebe. He doesn't seem angry with you, and, while driving skillfully with one hand, he makes you feel special by using the other to hold your hand, which rests on in your lap, on your wraparound skirt. Trying not to get mixed up in Steve's relationship with Nicholas, you say nothing, even though Steve's behaving immaturely, and Nicholas' face is red and swollen, as if he were crying, which he's not, though clearly he is miserable.

On the beach, you unwrap your skirt, and you're in your one-piece, black bathing suit. You rub sunscreen on your white, freckled arms and shoulders and thighs, and on Nicholas' white body. You and they have been to the beach together a few times, and Steve is the only one who's managed to work up a tan. The sunscreen smells sweet—like peaches and coconut—and reminds you of your childhood in the Coney Island neighborhood of Brooklyn. Somehow sand has already gotten mixed into the sunscreen, and you can feel yourself rubbing it into your skin. You'd like to remain in a reclining position on the hideous Thomas the Tank Engine towel (Ivan's) you've brought, because your body looks best that way—reclining; but you think you should help Nicholas and Steve build a giant sand castle. As soon as you start to help, by letting damp sand run down through your fist to be shaped into parapets, Steve says, "I think I'll take a swim." You suspect that maybe he's been taking you to the beach because he can't cope with being alone with Nicholas, and you help him take care of the kid. You watch Steve gracefully enter the surf, his body still trim from the carpentry, the physical labor he's doing.

Your legs are asleep, and you, full of sand, are bored. Steve shakes his wet hair over you, and you gasp at the coldness of the water drops. He laughs the laugh you remember from years ago, when you were both kids in college. He looks at you with his head tilted, as he always does, because he has a problem with his eyes—his eyeballs seem to tremble. But his gaze is intense, loving. You feel like part of a family here—Steve, you, Nicholas. You forget that you have a hideous ex out there, and a kid of your own who's seeing a therapist, and that Steve is only here in New York because he's on probation for doing something like selling drugs or hitting Bebe, and that Nicholas also is seeing a therapist. "My jail psychologist told me I tested sociopathic," Steve says.

He sits on your towel and begins to devour the chicken and honey mustard sandwiches you've made. "Bebe is marrying a lawyer in Denver—an ugly toad," he says. "Is that what's bothering you?" you ask. "Nothing's bothering me," he says, chewing. Drops from his hair drip into the sand, creating tiny little sand balls. "She's doing it for money and security," he says. You say nothing, happy to be taken into his confidence. This is Steve, opening up. "Are you jealous?" you ask. "No," Steve laughs. "I hate her so much." "Your hatred is ruining your life," you say. "Maybe you should try these visualization exercises to get rid of your hatred." You are doing visualization exercises, at that time, not in order to stop thinking about Steve, but in order to get money. The exercises are not exactly visualizations—they're supposed to be self-hypnosis, and the man who speaks extremely slowly on the tape tells you to imagine yourself in the sun, on a beach letting old hatreds, negative attachments, and envy leak out of you, while sunshine and golden relaxation begin to fill the void. "You deserve wealth," the man on the tape tells you. You are beginning to feel that you actually do deserve wealth. "I hate her so much that if she were here I'd drown her," says Steve.

Meanwhile, you feel yourself beginning to envy Bebe. She has Steve so much in love with her that he hates her. He thinks about her endlessly. He takes care of his son so she can go to law school. And she's going to marry an ugly lawyer for money and security. You find yourself wishing that Steve hated you as much as he hates Bebe.

# Icy Sedgwick

## The Thwarted Stalker

A fine rain spatters the streets of Ealing as he follows her to the train station. She holds the handle of a blue umbrella in one hand, and the hand of her boyfriend in the other. This is the first time he has seen him, but he does not like her boyfriend. He strains to hear their conversation, but he doesn't like to get too close. He only catches occasional words, and her laugh pierces the cold night air.

The station looms on the far side of the green, and their pace quickens. They cross the road, and she puts down her umbrella as they head into the station. He is not far behind, dodging the number 65 bus as he runs across the road. He curses mentally, reminding himself that he must still use the crossing. He ducks behind a pillar when he enters the station. He watches as she kisses her boyfriend goodbye, before passing through the barriers. The boyfriend waits until she disappears from sight onto the bridge to the platforms, when he turns and leaves the station.

He takes his chance and follows her.

She boards the train sitting at the platform, waiting to depart. He gets on further down the carriage, burrowing into his ample coat. He sneaks occasional glances at her, unable to believe that only a few yards separate him from her. She snuggles into her long black coat, before pulling a book from her Nintendo satchel. The bag strikes him as being too geeky for someone so beautiful, but he decides to let it pass. He squints, trying to see what book she is reading. The cover is black, with "Neil Gaiman" emblazoned in white. Her left hand blocks the title. He thinks he will pick up a copy tomorrow. Reading it himself will make him feel closer to her.

During the journey, he wonders how she cannot notice him looking. He even musters the courage to openly stare, but her book proves too engrossing. She looks up only as the train pulls into the station at Hammersmith. Standing up, she shoves the book into her bag and waits for the doors to open. He remains seated, waiting until she jumps down onto the platform. Once she heads up the stairs, he too leaps from the train and follows at a distance.

The rain has stopped, and the streets of Hammersmith are quiet. He takes extra care to hang back, to stay out of sight. He knows that he has every right to walk these streets and that if anyone asked, he could say his following her was purely coincidental, but he does not wish to draw any attention to himself. Not yet.

He follows her up the Shepherd's Bush Road, watching as the freezing wind catches the tail of her long coat and fans it out behind her. He feels his ears grow numb and he pulls his collar up around his neck, as if he could somehow blot out the cold. He wonders if she feels it, too. Halfway up the road, she pulls out a set of keys. She opens a large red door between a greasy spoon café and a 24-hour laundrette. His heart leaps into his mouth. He cannot believe that he now knows where she lives. He can begin to send her gifts. He is sure she will like them. Then she will love him.

He slows to a stroll and passes the door, hoping to spot the number. Disappointment hits him when he sees the intercom. Six flats lie beyond the door, and she could live in any one of them. True, he is closer to knowing where she lives than he has ever been, but he is not close enough. He peers at the intercom, wondering if the buzzers are attached to names. They are not—each buzzer is simply numbered, nothing more.

He steps back, hoping to see a light come on in one of the windows above. He thinks that it will give him a clue. He forgets about the flats at the back of the building. The rooms remain dark, the empty windows glaring down at him with disapproval. His heart sinks. He wonders if this is a sign. Perhaps she is not the one.

He shoves his hands in his pockets, and turns away. He pouts, feeling sullen. Head down, he trudges down the street, back towards Hammersmith. A woman coughs on the other side of the street. He looks up and sees the most beautiful woman in the world waiting at the bus stop. She wears a white coat, and her blonde hair is tucked into a white beret. He waits for a pause in the traffic and crosses the road, sidling up to the bus stop. She looks at him as he checks the bus timetable, but dismisses him as simply another commuter.

She stands up as the 220 to Wandsworth pulls up at the stop. He decides to follow her.

# Gail Louise Siegel

## Habit

Returning to her modest Chicago suburb from a weekend French class, Marguerite murmurs, "*Merci*" to the puzzled bus driver, who squints as she descends to her waiting husband.

Monday, she parks under the boughs of her dentist's magnolia in a gracious village, miles north of her own. Radio blaring, she angles her tires into the curb and sets the brake against a steep drop. She cuts the engine and whispers, "Goodbye" to the d.j. as if he's her lover.

Supine in a padded chair, under her dentist's cologned shadow, she blinks away sudden arousal. After ex-rays and floss, she rides the commuter train to work from his magnolia-shaded village.

There, the elevator jerks to a halt and its disembodied voice recites, "Floor twenty-two." Marguerite replies, "Thank you" to the vacant shaft.

She warms her morning coffee in the microwave. The display counts down from 25. As the 13 morphs to 12 she reaches out to dial her sister on the keypad.

She stirs in creamer with the tip of her ballpoint until a faint blue slick swirls up. She tosses that cup and brews another.

Each time she finishes a memo, she fights typing, "… and they all lived happily ever after."

At lunch, the Vietnamese clerk at the deli gives her an extra drumstick; Marguerite grips the warm paper sack and almost leans in to kiss her.

Back at work, her desk phone rings and she answers her cell, baffled by the silence until the desk unit *brrrriings* again.

Ending a call, her boss says, "See you tomorrow," and Marguerite nearly says, "I love you."

On the train home she dozes, snoring in spurts and waking up parched. She exits at her routine stop: an intersection of shabby and tidy. Marguerite shivers in the parking lot under the bleak cone of a streetlamp. She calls her husband and says her car has been stolen.

"Again," he says.

Marguerite pictures him zipping his nubby brown fleece, clicking on his headlights. She runs her tongue over dry front teeth. Then she remembers her dentist and the distant morning, when she parked on a hilly lane strewn with magnolia petals.

# Emeniano Acain Somoza

## My Lost Siquijor

Now, as the leader of the keeners drew her lungs out for the final bravura, mother pulled out her pristine handkerchief and, in the middle of that sonata, she blew her nose with a resounding honk, making it all the more vexatious for all spirits dead or, half-alive lurking there in the middle of our out-flung barrio; the housemaid who appeared from behind the heavy maroon drapery which divided the keening room and the pantry teetered bashfully on some imaginary beeline with a tray full of locally-brewed ales and home-baked cookies and waffles, was gloriously, gloriously affrighted by the cacophonic orchestration of the keeners' elegy and mother's nose-blow—the tray tilted to the left, glasses glided to that side, of course, disturbing the equilibrium; in an instant, the whole place was a mess—clinking glasses, girlish shrieks, and the sibilant susmarioseps of the toothless elderly. I closed my eyes. Mother half-aware of her little part in the melee tried to conceal her embarrassment by folding her handkerchief and dusting off the droplets of liquid on my repellent jacket. But when sooner she tried compulsively to wipe my face with the defiled hanky, I looked at her with a knowing look. She relented and whispered, "We'd better be going before the bamboo grove gets too dark."

After an intermittent series of leave-takings with the folks who according to my mother came mostly not to pay respects to the dead lady, Inday Vacion, but to catch up on the latest thread of controversy surrounding the cause of the death of this dame Salvacion Duhaylungsod, we trekked into one of the many mysterious nights in our lives as inhabitants of a remote barrio in the municipality of Larena on the island of Siquijor.

We traced our way back into the winding rugged trail and past the thick patch of ipil-ipil trees. Under the silky light of the full moon, the shadow of the leaves on the back of my hand looked like frail extremities of some non-earthlings squiggling deep into skin.

"What can you say about the dead lady's outfit? Don't you think it's rather outmoded? I mean, I will not be caught dead wearing that lacy frock!"

"Mother, how could you not be caught dead wearing an outmoded outfit like that if you're already dead?"

"Junior, I'm telling you this and I swear under the divine penumbra of this August moon, have a conscience if you please with your choices of clothes for your dead folks. You being the eldest of my ruffians of a brood."

The minute we stepped out into the meadow, I hailed a silent hosanna. Up in the sky, a dark cloud filtered the floodlight of the grayish moon. Just a few steps away, the bamboo grove was beckoning with the impenetrable beyondness of the otherworld.

"Ma! Look!" I hung on tight to her rubber belt as a cold wad of wind wafted by with a cold hand barely touching my nape. A dog's howl sliced into the silence. The bamboo grove creaked and while mother quickly pulled out something from her bag, the tallest of the clump bowed down before us.

"We can trace our steps back and take the feeder if we want to, but as the Holy Ghost is with us, we can pass by this witched place safe and unharmed." She said with a firm voice. The wind grew harsh.

She opened her Gideonite Bible. And before she could commence with her litany, the grass, as if moved by a higher order, lifted itself up and before us was a silver-white coffin with a candle at its head. I hugged my mother and closed my eyes.

"The Lord is my shepherd, I shall not want ..." so she began ...

\*

"Shoo! Get out of my sight, you spawn of unbelievers!" Old man, Silverio, my stepfather's father who was in the middle of some divination furiously drove my playmates away. The heckling youngsters scurried every which way at the sight of the naked old man hulking like a displeased turkey.

Known as the oldest living herbalist and spirit-conjurer in our barrio, I knew nothing could stop him from making that ritual even if mother showed signs of disapproval against such unscriptural spiritual ceremony. I knew it because I saw him secretly pouching a few grains of salt in the small room before I went to sleep. Before that I also overheard him pestering my stepgrandma for four one-centavo coins.

"This is for the good of your beloved boy. I told you it's beyond my wildest imagination why you have to give him away to a woman who has an English name for a god! And besides, what is there to make out of a marriage to a prefabricated mother? And do tell me, Pastora, how could you come to like her with that obnoxious boy of hers whose eyes always seem to burn with unmouthed expletives?"

"Ram your words back down your tonsils, old man! You know she could well be the last hope for your thug of a son! Besides, tell me, dear Silverio, who else in this barrio has got a wife who reads an English Bible, huh? Well why, she even reads it with her son eh ..."

"By our dead ancestors' name, I swear, the ritual has never been shunned away like a horrible plague. Only this woman, only this woman; but since you seem to have been hexed by her as to immensely favor her to be our dear Julito's wife, shush you old woman, nobody's going to stop me from laying down the necessary ingredients with the foundations of their planned house. Now get me another centavo. I lack one for the west direction."

"I will find one for you my king salmon…only you please, please promise not to go through it without your decent habiliments on. It's a shame to be doing it in the lowlands with those, uh, endowments of yours, you know … I swear it's a shame now. Besides I'm sure the spirits would consider for now … sure they would not take it against you if they see you spiffed up."

"Woman, what's all this sudden vituperation about my stuff, huh? Hush it. I shall do the ceremony as I please."

I was all drenched in sweat and squirming behind the dusty rattan hammock all throughout the short whispery verbal tussle. I didn't have to tell mother, of course, she seemed to know everything; so on second thoughts, I tipped on the incoming butt-show to my playmates, who waited hidden in the nearby bush of coronitas and cadena de amor.

"Shoo! Go back all you rascals to the woeful wombs of your heretic mothers!" The old man was mad.

A giant bat glided straight to the last unfelled tree in the middle of the lot where our future home was envisioned to grow.

*

So we lived in a small nipa hut built out of folk beliefs and rituals in the middle of a coconut plantation where my kid brother, Levis was born many many months later after we three – mother, my stepfather, and I - moved in at three in the morning at the behest of old master, Silverio. Three years later, when I was in grade four, wide-eyed, frail, and stringy-haired adopted sister Virgie joined us.

"Kids, you will treat her as if she's your own. Remember, she has been motherless all her life, and now she just lost a father; a word, a look could send her down the bog of depression... so, now listen, if I hear just a sob or see a track of tear on her cheek because one of you caused it, I will not spare a lashing from you...." Levis nodded. I thought it was rather uneventful to be having a girl around without a nag, a scream, or anything prissy.

"Are we communicating clearly about little Virgie's not-crying, Junior?" I naturally had to nod to that.

She was delicate as a dewdrop. Levis and I couldn't get through her. My stepfather, her full-blooded uncle, had a tough time with her. Mother was her only friend, spokesperson, interpreter, and refuge. I thought it was painful to be a girl. In time all of her defenses crumbled and she was sunny again. Her singlemost quirk which I found rather crumby was eating first the inside of a ripe guava before the soppy peelings.

Afternoons were always like this. First mother would gather us around her after finishing up whatever staple provision was set on our plastic plates. So there was Virgie, Levis, and me, Junior—reed-thin all three like praying mantises as she led the afternoon prayers before commanding us to sleep.

But that was long before I discovered that the world had two dimensions—the divine and the diabolic.

The first, pure and sacred, memories of it were set against a white backdrop of white shirts, my stepfather's white leather shoes, Virgie's frilly white dress and those white ribbonets, Levis' white belt, and mother's church hymnals covered with white paper which she recycled from those large waxy Chinese calendars.

Saturday was the official day of the divine plane with Jesus Loves Me as its music theme, which to my childish cerebration, sounded more elegiac than panegyric. I guessed it was due mostly to mother's vocal gymnastics that lilted along the untuneful pentatonic octave—tintinnabulatingly sopranic at its best, and gravelingly basso at its worst.

"Children, human beings are the only creatures gifted with a lot of faculties for praising the Lord. If you know you have the gift, hone it, then use it for His greater glory."

"Mother, there is no greater glory in singing without a gift."

"Look here, Junior, you would know you have the gift just by looking at how others close their eyes when you sing. I mean, have you often wondered how enrapt the whole parish had been since I started singing on top of my lungs?"

"Yes, mother. They wished some people would realize that some talents were not meant for public exhibition."

"At least I'm giving them a classical side show with my sopranic renderings."

"Mother, you're not actually admitting you were born for the circus, are you?"

"Hush, you giftless boy. Now kids, let's move on to our next exercise on blending.... You see ..."

*

Mother was a stylist of a dressmaker, which, as she would often tell us, was the most special of the gifts she had ever received from the Lord.

"Well, why, I had never walked in to any formal instruction just to learn it."

How she really made all those divine dresses for each and every customer fascinated me especially when I see them—even the most aristocratic of ladies in the high-end of our local caste system—daintily slithering into a dress cut and sewn by her. When I told her she could actually use some focusing on this one special gift instead of displaying teeth, tongue and tonsils in church, she sent me out to gather firewood in the forest so that I would learn to listen to the birdsongs, which according to her were just as God-inspired as hers. I eventually stopped bugging her.

On days when the sun was up and yellow wrens twittered on top of our sagging eaves, I would see her tinkering with some man's craft, say metallurgy, which was a bit dangerous because she would be setting fire here and there while warning us kids not to come close to her within a ten-meter radius with that ubiquitous twig for a whip.

And on such days, too, I was the object of the world's most stinging lashes, some scars are so stubborn a million baths in the river or the sea could not bring them to a complete healing, or worse, forgetting because along with them are memorable snippets of my childhood.

"Come Levis, let's go take a short dip before we go home. A little cooling would not be bad eh. What do you think?" I was trying to cajole him into swimming without mother's permission.

"I will not be getting one of her lashings anymore, Manoy. You can't tag me along on a bite of your slimy toffee."

"Yes you will come with me as I say. Besides who will look after you if you go ahead? Guess what, the bamboo grove is a little shady today … you reckon, little brother?"

"Err … I will not!"

"Yes you will! Here now, let's go for a short swim without dipping our heads into the water. That way we won't be giving mother a start … Brilliant idea eh?"

That day, an hour after lunchtime, on a hillock overlooking the sea, and while a seagull was gearing up for a nose-dive, I received my first soul-splitting lashing that left me with an indelible scar on my left leg.

*

Summers came breezing in with the scent of promise of freedom from the rigors of classroom works. Each one was always a time to temporarily abandon academic fetters and bury grudges toward a regimenting system along with its pedantic implementers inside our recycled school net-bags.

Fortunately, mother always made sure ours looked presentable—denim patches here and there, depending on wherever the frayed part was. Eventually, our school bags transformed into psychedelic quilts—of swatches of fabrics, of our nothingness, and of our dreams.

"Mother, school year ends next week. Reynaldo, the principal's son gets the second honors and Mr. Maglinte is allegedly going to take him to a trip to the far and big city for a prize."

"I bet he is going to buy his son the whole island if he gets your honors. Oh let them do whatever they fancy."

"Uhm, mother, it's not that…."

"You are not going to let him beat you into it, are you?"

"Mother, I was just wondering if you could also mete out a reward system for us. I mean, I want a real school bag this time. For J. D. Salinger's sake, mother, this is my fifth first honors."

She looked at me like I was big and strong enough a man already. Then she hugged me.

"Junior, just because you are inches taller than me now doesn't mean you cannot carry that cute bag-quilt of yours. Didn't I tell I will get you a real one when you are in the high school already? Okay, let's split it. You raise the ten pesos, I will shoulder the other half. Deal, huh?"

I choked down half of the despair, but I smiled on the other for the flicker of hope. Yes, I could have a real school bag at last.

"Wait. What kind of bag does this friend of yours wear to school?"

"Friend?"

"Yes. This J.D. Sali— does he brandish it to you like it's the most precious thing there is in this world? I'll tell you what ... a person who pesters you with something, say, a bag, just so you can keep up with him has no genuine friendly intentions."

I wiped off the scowl on my face with a smile. Then I hugged my mother tight. That very moment, next to my obsession with a school bag, mother was the best thing I ever held close to my heart. I saw her eyes filming with tears as she withdrew to the kitchen.

The piece of sky I saw from my window was a calming soft blue as night slowly broke out into the horizon. A few minutes passed, Virgie signaled supper.

I thought it was a rather fancy supper. I was surprised. Instead of the usual fare of green leafy vegetables and unpolished rice, mother opened the last can of sardines she had kept behind the big earthen jar. I knew it was spared for the visit of church elder. At the table, my stepfather proudly announced my scholastic achievement. Then everybody feasted like mad on the sardines until we all forgot about the little gardens of green leafy vegetables we had grown inside our stomachs.

\*

We were running barefoot now on the powder-white sands of our shoreline past the estuary that divided our barrio and the next going up north. The sea was an endless field of metal slivers sparkling under the noon sun. A solitary gull shot upwards and in seconds it darted swiftly down into the sea. In a moment, a fish was wiggling at its beak.

A kingfisher perched on a rock. I stopped and tiptoed towards it as a picture of a bird in a cage swung before me. I was inches closer now when a pebble whizzed past it. I threw an angry look at the culprit.

Behind our backs were sacks heavy with our finds—trash from people's junk pits which we would sell to scrap dealers. I was proud of my merchandize as a ten-peso bill wadded in my mind.

Coming in from the sea, it always felt like we were some pirates or bandits pillaging through villages for precious metal scraps, bottles, cans and tins. First, we would spread ourselves into a chosen village, rummage into their backyards, then zero in on their garbage cans, and finally sacking whatever we deemed marketable.

Excitedly, I took to the open backyard of a concrete house. To my right, a hammock was still in the shade of an ancient acacia. I found it rather unusual. Nobody was stirring. The air was as ominously still as the deadly sigh of a ghost town.

I slowly headed to the heap of junks by the giant metal water tank. I was disappointed. I only found two empty cans of milk. Suddenly, my eyes caught sight of bottles, hundreds or a thousand of them stocked behind the outhouse. My heart jumped. I struck good luck.

I figured a sacking of six or seven of the bottles wouldn't be too much of a loot considering that a dozen or two looked like they were intentionally smashed. Besides I hurt my right foot with a shard of glass. So I thought of adding one for the injury.

"Ruelito? What are you doing with my bottle?" It almost slipped off my hand.

"G-good afternoon, Ma'am.... I'm s-sorry.... I can e-explain...."

"No need! Get out of my yard! Go home, you filthy son of a scavenger!"

\*

Inday Vacion, or Miss Salvacion Duhaylungsod, still looked witchy and waspy in a lacy frock and even with make-up. Her face, waxy gray, bore the burden of bitterness towards a world she thought would mourn sincerely for her passing.

She was wrong in many ways. For instance, a huddle of mothers was close to celebrating her death because she had allegedly caused the sufferings and anguish of their children.

"I know Salvacion is death's most priceless collection now."

"Ladies, let the lovelorn find true happiness now. Let her pass you by with nary a grudge. We the feeling should be happy now for our dear children."

I was with mother who insisted that I should pay respects to the dead.

"My son, death is the arbiter of enmities. There is no use in nursing ill thoughts when your enemy is already dead. Come now, let's take a look at how she handled death."

"She looks like she is grimacing in pain, mother. Was death unkind to her?" I whispered.

"I cannot exactly tell myself, but I think you are right. Given her ... expression, I think death gave her a hell of a time. Or it could just be the frock. I'm not really sure. It just kind of added to the ugliness of death."

I remembered the deceased wearing that lacy frock during our United Nations celebration in school. Her class was assigned by the principal to represent Spain, ours our own country. The whole school paraded through the dusty trails of the barrio with our respective national costumes. In the middle of the production, Miss Duhaylungsod, terror teacher in the highest order, looked like a bantam fowl swell for fiesta banquet. A week after the celebration, she left her lover for two years, Mr. Sitti Jainal, a certified womanizer who was rumored to have fathered all of the Turkish-looking kids in town.

The frock now also reminded me of her other favorite dress she wore in school on the first day of classes after that summer of rummaging through people's junkyards.

It was in our Home Economics class where I first experienced a heartless act of humiliation. Her words stung me more painfully than the shard of glass that injured my foot that summer.

"Class, we have a saying that one cannot expect to grow berries out of tomato seeds. If you have a whore for a mother, naturally you'd bear a son who would grow up to be a problem citizen in the future no matter how intellectually gifted he may be. I am telling you this because one of you dared to steal some of my belongings right from my backyard last summer."

Everybody was edgy. I was crashed.

"You hold your horses! I have made peace with the Lord already. I trust He will avenge for me.... So, now tell me, what dish did you try to cook last summer...?"

I came home teary-eyed. I wanted to tear the school bag into pieces, but I thought of the other ten pesos mother paid for … my recycled quilt-bag … the gardens in our stomachs … my dreams....

"Junior, are those tears in your eyes? How terribly do you miss your teacher?" Mother's nudge brought me back to the wakeful realm of the living.

"Good god, mother, no! I just feel sleepy. Can we go now?"

"Let's wait until the vigil is over. I just wanted to take a bite or two on Inday's famous cookies. I was told it was her cookies that had endeared her to Mr. Jainal. That I should find out myself."

Now as the leader of the keeners drew her lungs out for the final bravura, mother pulled out her pristine handkerchief and, in the middle of that pestiferous sonata, she blew her nose with a resounding honk, making it all the more vexatious for all spirits dead, or half-alive lurking there in the middle of our out-flung barrio....

# Girija Tropp

## Godmother of Trash

The late summer takes back its warmth and the birds seem uncaring about our mangy neighbourhood cat, interested as they are in the rubbish I bring out of the house in an unending stream. My son and I will be moving into a rent-control by the end of the year and in the mean time I soft-renovate other people's homes in exchange for free accommodation. I prefer if the owners take a long holiday but in this one the couple decided to stay, and the husband is no gift. Not that he is out of line but there is something off-kilter. He wants to be involved, and his decisions rule to the extent that I wonder why they hired me.

A magpie skids around the garage corner on one set of bird claws like it's been warned to get here in time. The curiosity of the non-human world is constant, and grudging; paper crumples in a reproachful murmur, electrical cords refusing to fold down into the skip corner. By the time I am done, the sun has fallen off my neck and off to woo another.

The husband organises to take me for a breakfast meeting to choose curtain colours. He is having a lean meat salad and crème caramel, an odd breakfast choice. In the house before the last, the son's girlfriend was taken out by his dad in a platonic ménage à trois. He told us at the dinner table that the girl had problems with relationships and he was helping out. What he said next blew me away. He said that he told her that she had a fear of penetration. *Euu*, I said inaudibly to my soup. The family continued to pass the salt, talking about the dad's immersion days in the Reichian model of therapy. This one who is buying me breakfast analyses me too.

You are highly strung but I like that about you.

I think of cables on telephone wires. Even as he speaks he displays a severe interest in a woman walking past.

Ah, I say, as if we totally understand what his words mean. I believe I am hard on men in general but do I want to change that? Why throw out a defective when one could choose well in the first place? Still, I wonder if I am the defective one but that kind of thinking is stressful and so let me avoid it.

The trees on the street lean in the same direction as the woman who has now crossed the road and is talking on her phone. When I look closer, I see that the angled branches try to lean this way too.

# Donna D. Vitucci

## Rupture

The dad sat on his patio and sipped his early evening cocktail, minding his girls as they played in the yard turning gloomy. Neela and Coco, they were, with names like gorilla baby names, and with the sweet malleable mugs gorillas have before they elongate, grow second teeth, puff up linebacker-ish in breadth and swagger. He could locate them by their screams, by their sing-songing. They played under the apple tree, stealing the apples—but not those really rotten and liquefying—from the September bees, accruing a little bomb shelter stockpile. The game they played they called Armo-Get-On. They watched too much doomsday TV.

They plopped the apples in the wheelbarrow, each took a handle, serious about their jobs and transportation. As they wobbled their produce around the side between houses, the backyard accepted a film of peace. Until the teenager next door—the side not with the girls wheelbarrow-ing the apples—started pitching his knives. The dad heard weapons thwapping, sticking the side of the neighbor's wood shed, and the kid missing, the kid cursing. Tattoos and weightlifting in the garage. Now knives. The kid was perfecting all his circus angles.

The dad sipped, and then upended the ice to rattle down and clink his teeth. The side of the house was in shadow and his girls could not be seen. Or heard. And this set off his boozy-woozy alarm. On the goth-boy side, knives graced the grass, innocent tossed play things. The dad circled the whole of his house outside, carrying his empty cocktail. His girls and the boy had vanished. The drink in him said, "Ran away with the circus."

A kalliope or an ice cream truck played music in the street. A lion or a greyhound trotted at the end of a leash. The man waved his glass to the dog walker, who did not emerge from behind the ice cream truck. The manhole cover in the middle of the street had been shifted to reveal the sewer.

A field full of bees swarmed the man's backyard. They were lifting the apple tree. They were that many and that strong and that determined. They could lift little girls hunched in a big metal wheelbarrow and strong man knife throwers and women lion tamers. The bees were eager to increase their throng, and changing the shapes of things as they did.

The girls would learn to trapeze in skimpy, spanglely outfits against all child labor and laws of decency. Before this night they had only ever hung upside down by their bent knees from the lowest apple tree branch. Soon they would rocket through air. They would learn timing.

While the dad cricked his neck tilting up at the sky, wondering how they'd got away from him, who put his girls up there and made them stars, and how they would get down, Neela and Coco forgot they ever had a dad, or a place to return to, other than the silver bar advancing and receding, metronome teaching them the word "rely" in a world without a net. Show business names they brought with them like lucky pennies in their shoes. At the end of their act each night, their ballerina feet poised fifth position in the sawdust and the sublime, they held hands to bow. Their noses touched their knees. They had always been so flexible. Eyes shiny as wet stones, hair lustrous as moonlight, they folded in half.

The gorillas inside their cages gave up furious, muscular applause. A lion roared and the woman tossed it an extra large dog biscuit. The kalliope sang Don't Sit under the Apple Tree, and all the town's children stirred in their dreams. Where the trailers had been parked among cinders, knives crowded into one place perpendicular, and the boy, pale without his makeup but painted on his limbs, pulled them free of the tree bark, as his arms had grown stronger and his aim more accurate. His upper lip predicted a ring master's moustache, and a time when all things would buckle to his whip.

A bearded man hummed among the tents in his janitor-like way. He carried a push-broom for a prop. Unless you drew close you wouldn't know he wore a beard of bees to hide a weak and negligible chin. Huddling up and hugging his face, the hive operated as one wide wing, caressing where whiskers refused to grow. In their bee-hungry hearts, relishing their sting, they knew Neela and Coco wasted allergic. Those girls—collecting sappy apples among bees, the initial mistake, and their flying through the firmament merely an irritating delay.

Neela and Coco were paper-thin, they walked an origami path, they folded themselves flat as the alphabet. The circus celebrated contortionists, but what those girls could do was out of this world.

Tomorrow's headline already set in 46 point: *Another Negligent Father?* And in smaller type: *Authorities are investigating.*

A Child Protective Services spokesperson said, in its best blend of active and passive, "We are reviewing our field notes to see what might have been missed on our last visit."

The dad's rebuttal by telephone interview: "I do what I can as a lone parent."

"Those girls were hot from the get-go," said an anonymous neighbor who wished to remain so. "They glowed in their bassinets. What collected in their diapers scorched." Fueling speculation the speaker had once been the girls' babysitter.

"Their Hoochie Mama left us," the dad said in another feel-sorry-for-me statement. He couldn't catch a break from the crowd.

The vendor behind the scratched-up plasti-glass of the ice cream truck said, "They had star quality." He cited grubbiness his reason for not lifting the window for better auditory. A few said he needed a shave and others said the compressor keeping the end-of-the-season ice cream cold inside buzzed like a son-of-a-gun.

The lady next door denied she ever gave birth. Her greyhound posed on the patio slab regally, squinted his eyes at the backyard while she stroked its hatchet-sized head. She said, "What boy?"

# Zachary Watterson

## The Prophet

Hershel scooped rocky road ice cream into plastic bowls, and set the bowls on the counter for the schizophrenics to take. One of them, a man named Zook, who wore grease-stained jeans and a button-down orange shirt, scrubbed dishes an arm's length from where Hershel stood. Zook's jacket, something he washed about twice yearly, and then only with staff prompting, lay somberly on the kitchen tiles, its cotton fur-lined collar sopping up suds that ran down Zook's forearms and dripped off his elbows onto the floor.

Residents queued one behind the other, maybe a quarter of the sixty that lived in the halfway house. Ice cream was a big hit, and it only got served for snack on Tuesdays, the evening after the Sysco truck delivered the ten-gallon container, as well as other less exotic food stuffs, such as pasta, salt, liver, onions, and all matter of cheap edibles. As Hershel served scoop after scoop, he glanced down at the others in the queue. Chun-Wei rocked on the balls of his feet, Linden drooled on his shirt, and Esther tapped her nails against her teeth.

Out of the corner of his line of vision, Hershel spotted a four-inch critter walking along the wall, legs acting like little plungers on the scum-slick wall, slick from so much steam, sweat, and moisture made by frying, simmering, and boiling things, and slick from the wet northwest breezes that drifted in from the often-open living room door. Sometimes, when he wanted to be funny while talking with friends, Hershel compared these roaches to Chihuahuas, those tiny nuisances with that annoying, high-pitched bark. Sometimes he laughed at his own jokes harder than anyone else did. But just now, with the roach crawling along at eye-level, he didn't find it so funny. He grabbed a spatula from an upright container brimming with large serving spoons and the like. And he swatted the roach dead. The thwack of the spatula hitting the roach and the wall was sickening. The roach fell to the floor.

"You killed the prophet!" Zook said.

Hershel looked at the small, dirty man, and blinked.

"Why did you do that?" Zook's unshaven cheeks flushed. He breathed fast and hard, and his eyes flashed with anger.

Hershel considered explaining to Zook why he had killed the roach. But he also realized they had a fundamental difference of opinion about the critter he had killed.

"Tell me," Zook said. "How do you know that wasn't the prophet?"

"I don't."

Zook nodded. "OK, then." And with that, Zook turned back to the sink and began scrubbing spoons.

Hershel's shift didn't end until eleven p.m., and although Zook, by washing snack dishes, had earned a cupful of loose-leaf tobacco, Zook didn't approach the office. For the remainder of his shift, Hershel sat listlessly under fluorescent lighting in the office, considering the fine line separating the insane from the sane.

# Kulpreet Yadav

## All You Need is One Good Shot

If you look out of the window for a moment, ignoring the dead man on the floor, you'll be greeted by the nature at its best—it's springtime.

The sky is bluer than the bluest you have seen in the just wound-up winter, and the flowers are a riot of colour in the small garden. But if you look closely, and in the nick of time, you may spot in the river beyond the garden, a boat with the figure of a man in it.

Is he fishing, you wonder?

Has he seen the murderer?

Before you decide to use the binoculars, you hear a plop. It's rather loud and comes from behind. You turn and observe that a small portion of plaster has fallen off the wall. It takes less than a second for the panic to set in and you duck out of reflex. The air starts to thin around you. For the first time since arriving in the room half an hour earlier, you realize that it's too hot.

You begin to sweat and now your breathing gets labored too.

Visiting the crime scene alone was a mistake. Why did you ignore your assistant's warnings? More importantly, why did you join the police two years ago?

The boat has started its engines and the sound is getting louder. The gun is coming for you. You can't see the man in the boat, but you can hear the engine.

Of course you know the dead man had many enemies. He was a lawyer and people said he cared about the truth. Something you are not sure you do anymore.

But the doubt is momentary. Your father was a policeman. You recall the oath you took at the Police Academy. You take three long breaths, remove your wallet and flip it open. Dressed in a crisp khaki police uniform you have your arm around your wife's shoulder. On her wrist she is wearing the gold bracelet you had gifted her last Diwali. You both are smiling.

The man in the boat has killed the engines. You pause and hear the boat's bow lap the river water. You crawl from under the window and curve past the dead man. His eyes are open and you meet him in the eyes, but just for a second, before deciding to move on. The Glock is now out in your hands. You know the range is 50 meters and the magazine is full. You have 17 rounds, but all you need is one good shot.

You get up, press your back against the wall and strain all your senses. There is no sound now. In the present situation, your chances of survival are 50-50. You think of calling the back-up. But they will take minimum twenty minutes.

You are waiting, your wife's smile in your head and the pistol ahead of you, when the door opens. You hear a woman scream and a shot is fired.

*

It's dark and your head is throbbing as you open your eyes. You feel as if your body is moving; no, you are in a vehicle that's in motion. You extend your hands, but can't. The pressure on the wrists suggests that you have been restrained. The moment of the scream comes back to you. You had wanted to fire, but couldn't, because the person who entered the room was a woman. You have been a gentleman, someone used to respecting women. She had screamed and as you lost that crucial window of a fraction of a second, she had fired. You had been hit on your shoulder, on the left side. The shock had knocked you out. Though you are awake now, you feel dizzy, perhaps because you have lost a lot of blood. The vehicle stops and the tires skid on the gravel. So she has brought you into the country. But why would she do that, you wonder?

The bonnet opens, but you close your eyes and feign to be unconscious. Two rough hands lift your legs and you are yanked out in two heaves and finally when you topple outside, the ground you hit is hard. Stones pierce into your body and the back of your head. An electric impulse cuts across but you resist somehow the temptation to scream. The rough hands once again grab your legs and another set of hands, which are smoother, lift you from the shoulders. No one is talking as you imagine a farmhand and a city-bred person, perhaps educated, take you along.

You count the steps and after sixty they stop and drop you. This time the fall is comfortable. But the smell suggests that perhaps you are in an animal shed. You hear footsteps walking away and you wait wondering if is safe to open your eyes.

When you open them you see a woman standing in front of you. Did you fall asleep, pretending to be lifeless? She has her hands on her hips and a cigarette is dangling from her mouth. You can't see her face as her back is towards the door, the only source of light, but can see the fire at the end of the cigarette and the smoke rising above her head.

'What do you want from me?' You whisper, meekly, not out of fear, but out of genuine inquisitiveness. You have always been fair in life, at school, in college and also as a policeman.

She laughs in return and you recognize her. She is your wife. 'Tina?'

She steps forward and opens the rope before sitting down next to you and pressing your head in her lap. She gently soothes your hair and whispers that she loves you. You give in to the darkness happily. You have no idea if your wife has saved your life when you had fallen asleep, or she is the one who had got you kidnapped and now you are dying due to the lack of medical attention.

If you ever wake up you will be happy to live in the world again with your wife. And if you die, you are happy to be dying in the arms of your lover.

You are the winner.

# CODA

# Laura Jensen

## WHAT THE DORMOUSE SAID: TAKE TIME TO READ, IT IS THE FOUNTAIN OF WISDOM

("White Rabbit" by Jefferson Airplane and "Take Time," an Inspirational Card)

### 1. A MOMENT OF DIALOGUE

There is an arch over a stage that separates the actors from the audience. When the actors stand at the base of the arch, they can address the audience directly. This tradition is called Proscenium Arch. A strong example of the proscenium arch is the 1950s television comedy *The Burns and Allen Show*.

In early July 2010 Laura Jensen browsed through the Architecture books at Tacoma Public Library and found *Apartments and Dormitories*, collected *Architectural Digest* articles from Dodge Press, 1958. She was reminded of *The Burns and Allen Show* by the black-and-white photographs and floor plans. (Prose: from Prosa oratio, speech going straight ahead: Origins, Eric Partridge)—Can we turn Proscenium Arch around, turn all of the prose of an essay into a direct address to the audience just by adding a moment of dialogue? Laura Jensen lived at a dormitory as illustrated in black-and-white photographs in *Apartments and Dormitories*. When she lived there she was called upon once to speak.

April 26, 1968—it was a fine reading. Galway Kinnell and Denise Levertov read. As the sun lowered Laura started back. She realized she had not planned the bus ride back and would have to walk. When dark came she was in a shopping center parking lot, the University Village.

Because the Village was in a valley by the University, the lighted picture windows of high rise dorms seemed very high. As she gazed at the distant windows, a vehicle, it was a police car, spun in the dark from behind the dark buildings.

An officer looked from the open car window, insisted she explain herself.

It was not trespassing to be on the parking lot when dark had fallen. Was it? All the cars were gone. Laura said she had been to a poetry reading.

That seemed to make it worse and worse.

Laura had believed the policeman was her friend. Laura thought then, the policeman was not her friend. That created an ugly shock that never changed back again. The street was ugly then. The policeman did not like her.

She walked up 45th, a long viaduct uphill to the campus. She walked along the chain link fence with evergreen shrubs that was the edge of the campus, to the narrow opening in the fence that led past the nice bricks of the dorm in the dark to the dorm entrance, to her floor on the elevator. Home at last. On the door was a sign she had made, lines from "The Skaters" by John Ashbery.

*Happier once again, for tomorrow is already here.*

## 2. Be A Lawyer

Sometimes things look different when you copy them down. If you wish to act as your own lawyer, be a lawyer. Laura Jensen, at a point as an adult, carefully wrote down this part of a lecture. A moment after she wrote it, she read it. She realized it meant something different from what she had assumed. It meant that only a lawyer should act as their own lawyer. It is somewhat sad that the article from *Apartments and Dormitories* calls to mind for Laura Jensen the story about the freshman dorm—sad because we know the policeman is our friend.

We can imagine a comment by George Burns about the book *Apartments and Dormitories*: George Burns: In the earlier scene, where Gracie moved the book marks ahead because she had been too busy to do her reading? Gracie is quite a reader. She found a book about *Apartments and Dormitories* and she said one dormitory looked like a horse show performance arena. She could not figure out where they had the service elevator with all the bleacher-style staircases. I gave her the magnifying glass. With that many units, there has to be an elevator.

*Apartments and Dormitories* includes an *Architectural Digest* article from 1953 about a dormitory at Tempe. Such housing must have been a stage some of the time to *Salt River Review*. When computer screens at the dormitory opened to the blue- and white-lettered poetry magazine, peripheral text books as well as student dialogue and writing became proscenium narrative. (Laura has looked through internet photos at ASU, these narrate a peripheral reality to the material on the screen at *Salt River Review*.)

### 3. Architectural Theme

At the dormitory, there had been no place to paint. At home, before college, Laura painted in her room, where the linoleum did not matter. But it was never spoken of. Laura's roommate had been a friend of hers for years. During summer vacation 1968, her roommate once drove two masonite boards to Laura's house from the lumber yard on the roof of her car and helped Laura carry them up the two turns of the narrow stairwell to her room.

Laura Jensen uses public transportation, walks or rides a bicycle. She passes white painted fences that her high school bus passed and remembers mist in the autumn morning, at the fence there were horses. Zoning allowed horses in that area then. On the bicycle Laura realized the dorm from *Apartments and Dormitories* has the rails and arena of a horse show. The Tempe dormitory metal fence is like the horse fence at the Fairgrounds.

There must have been an architectural theme for the dormitory where she plugged in the clock radio her mother gave her once for Christmas, punched out the window screen, "More air!" She looked through the binoculars her father gave her once for Christmas. The view, according to the 1962 map from the Seattle World's Fair, was a cemetery.

And the architectural theme must have been the elevator. On the map a picture of the Space Needle elevator rose up a narrow line one could imagine was the center of the curved supports seven hundred feet up, visible from a great distance at the approach to Seattle, on the skyline. Yes it was. The architectural theme of that dormitory was the elevator.

### 4. The Audience

It was at a Unitarian Church where a poetry reading would be that beautiful spring day. Laura took the bus early to explore. It had not occurred to her in general, although she had seen Mark Strand read, that it was intended that the audience heard poetry read aloud to them and were entertained, but that the reading was a chance for the audience to see the author of the poetry book.

Laura wore ordinary pale jeans with a cotton jacket and a triangle scarf. Galway Kinnell and Denise Levertov gave a fine reading. Denise Levertov wore a knit dress of dark and rose colors on a dark surface, red and rose fluorescent, A-line, long sleeves, no collar. As she began, she saw someone in the audience.

"Eve! Eve Triem!"

Far back in the pews, Laura was put off. She was dimly scandalized that an audience member was exposed, helpless, seated, not the one to speak, but called out loud.

*

*(Eve Triem grew up in San Francisco. Her poems were published in anthologies and magazines, and in her six books of poetry. The wife of writer Paul Ellsworth Triem, they moved to Seattle in the early nineteen-sixties. The small press Dragon Gate of Seattle and Port Townsend published Eve Triem's* New As A Wave: A Retrospective 1937–1983 *in 1984, when the author was eighty-two years old. Listed on the internet with her papers at University of Washington Special Collections is Correspondence with Denise Levertov: 1970–1972 and 1975–1980.)*

# CONTRIBUTORS' BIOGRAPHIES

**Liz Ahl** is the author of the chapbooks *A Thirst That's Partly Mine* (Slapering Hol, 2008), *Luck* (Pecan Grove Press, 2010), and *Talking About The Weather* (Seven Kitchens Press, 2012). She lives in New Hampshire.

**Pamela Alexander** is the author of four collections of poetry, the most recent of which is *Slow Fire* (Ausable/Copper Canyon). She taught writing for many years at MIT and Oberlin College, and is now exploring North America in an RV, writing nonfiction and fiction as well as poetry. See her at pamelaalexander.info and on Facebook.

**Roberta Allen** is the author of eight books and a visual artist in the collection of The Metropolitan Museum of Art. robertaallen.com

Mark Strand's version of "Interpretation of December" was first reprinted [after appearing in the fourth issue of *Porch*] in a volume of **Carlos Drummond de Andrade**'s *Selected Poems*, published in 1986, a year before the poet's death, with a number of additional translations by Thomas Colchie and Elizabeth Bishop. This poem from the 1940s is part of a series in which Drummond looks back at his childhood and the life of his family.

**Jay Baruch**'s collection of short fiction, *Fourteen Stories: Doctors, Patients, and Other Strangers* (Kent State University Press, 2007) was Honorable Mention in the short story category in *ForeWord Magazine*'s 2007 Book of the Year Awards. *What's Left Out*, his new collection of short fiction, is forthcoming from Kent State University Press. He's an Associate Professor of Emergency Medicine at the Alpert Medical School at Brown University, where he serves as the director of the Program in Clinical Arts and Humanities. "A Little Heart" copyright © 2007 by The Kent State University Press. Reprinted with permission.

**Gaston Baquero** was born in Cuba in 1918 and died in Madrid, Spain in 1997. He studied to be an agronomist, but early contact with José Lezama Lima and others turned his interests toward poetry and journalism. After the Cuban revolution, the island became untenable for Baquero, and he stopped writing poetry until he was officially exiled to Spain in 1959. His *Poesía completa* was published posthumously, and the editor of that volume, Pio É. Serrano, has written that Baquero is now "the most influential poet of new generations of poets in Cuba. Within him was always the impassioned heartbeat of his island...."

**Johannes Beilharz**, born 1956, writes in German and English, paints and translates. His most recent books are *101* (haiku and fibonacci poems) and *Eine finnische Jazznummer für die Missverstandenen* (poems, German), both published in 2014. He lives in Rome, Italy, and Pliezhausen, Germany.

**Mario Benedetti** (1920–2009), Uruguayan, but often considered a Spanish poet. Baptized with five names, according to Italian tradition: Mario Orlando Hamlet Hardy Brenno. Though little known to Anglophones, he was one of the most respected, popular, and prolific writers of Latin America. He published eighty books. *Rincón de haikus* [Haiku Corner] was published in 1999.

**James Bertolino** has twice won the *Quarterly Review of Literature* book publication prize, as well as the Discovery Award. His twelfth volume of poetry, *Ravenous Bliss: New and Selected Love Poems*, was published in 2014 by MoonPath Press, and individual poems have been reprinted in 41 anthologies. He retired from a position as Writer in Residence at Oregon's Willamette University in 2006, and lives with artist / poet Anita K. Boyle near Bellingham, Washington.

**Ankur Betageri** (b. 1983) is a poet, short fiction writer and visual artist based in New Delhi. He is presently Assistant Professor of English at Bharati College, University of Delhi.

**Charles Blackstone** is the author of the novels *Vintage Attraction* and *The Week You Weren't Here* and co-editor of *The Art of Friction*, an anthology. He currently serves as managing editor of *Bookslut* and lives in New York City.

**Pēters Brūveris** was born in Riga in 1957 and died in 2011. During that time, he published nine collections of poetry—among them: *Black Thrush, Red Cherries* (1987), *Amber Skulls* (1991), and *Sitting On A Park Bench* (1994)—as well as books of poetry for children, librettos and song lyrics, and texts for animation films. Brūveris was considered the best poet of his generation in Latvia: his work has a breadth of experience, global scope, backed by his studies of and translations from Latin, Turkish, Azerbaijani, the Crimean Tatar language, Lithuanian, Russian, Germany, and Prussian.

**Michael Burkard**'s most recent book is *lucky coat anywhere* (Nightboat Books). Three books of drawings and writings are available from blurb.com.

**Lee Byrd** lives in El Paso. In 1985, with her husband, poet Bobby Byrd, she founded Cinco Puntos Press, a publishing house recognized for its bilingual and multicultural books for children, young adults and adults. Lee has published a collection of short stories, *My Sister Disappears* (SMU Press), two children's books, *The Treasure on Gold Street* and *Lover Boy* (Cinco Puntos) and a novel, *Riley's Fire* (Algonquin), named one of the Top Ten Best Books of 2006 by *People* magazine.

**Becky Byrkit** lives and writes in Scottsdale and Flagstaff, Arizona. She performs with "[Becky Byrkit. poet, and the] Actual Musicians' Band." She teaches memoir and poetry at Arizona State University.

**Wendy Taylor Carlisle** lives and works in the Arkansas Ozarks. She is the author of two books of poetry and three chapbooks; most recently, *Persephone on the Metro* (MadHat Press, 2014). Her work has been nominated for the Pushcart Prize nine times. Some of her publications are linked at wendytaylorcarlisle.com.

**Rochelle Cashdan**, a former anthropologist, nowadays cultural journalist, lives in Guanajuato, Mexico after 33 years in the Pacific Northwest. Her speculative fiction, poetry and ethnic stories fan out from her own experience. Besides *SRR*, she has published in *Contemporary World Poetry*, *Big Pulp*, *Bewildering Stories*, and other online magazines.

**Tania Casselle**'s fiction has also appeared in *New York Stories*, *Saint Ann's Review*, *South Dakota Review*, *Carve*, *Quick Fiction*, *The Bitter Oleander*, the anthology *Harlot Red* (Serpent's Tail Press), and elsewhere. Originally from London, UK, Tania now lives in New Mexico. A long-time journalist, she writes for magazines around the world and also offers online writing seminars and editing/coaching services for writers.

**Alex Cigale**'s own English-language poems have appeared in the *Colorado*, *Green Mountains*, *North American*, and *The Literary Reviews*, and his translations of Russian Silver Age and contemporary poetry and prose in *Cimarron Review*, *Literary Imagination*, *Modern Poetry in Translation*, and other journals. A 2015 NEA Literary Translation Fellow for his work on Mikhail Eremin, from 2011 until 2013 he was Assistant Professor at American University of Central Asia in Bishkek, Kyrgyzstan.

**Peter Cooley** has published nine books of poetry, eight of them with Carnegie Mellon, that press just releasing *Night Bus To The Afterlife*. He has poems in recent issues of *The New Yorker*, *Plume*, *Conte*, *Missouri Review*, and other magazines. He is Senior Mellon Professor of English and Director of Creative Writing at Tulane.

**Flavia Cosma** is an award-winning Romanian-born Canadian poet, author and translator. She has published to date thirty-six books of poetry, narrative and children's literature. Her work has been represented in numerous anthologies in various countries and languages. Flavia Cosma is the director of the International Writers' and Artists' Residency, Val-David, Quebec, Canada and the President of the Biannual International Festivals at Val-David.

**Pablo Antonio Cuadra** (b. 1913) composed *Seven Trees Against the Dying Light*, the book which includes his long poem, "The Mango Tree," during the aftermath of the Sandinista uprising against the Somoza dynasty in Nicaragua in 1978–79. The poem's hero, Captain Cespedes de Aldana, is one of Cuadra's ideal characters, one who brought the first clock and the first mango tree to Mesoamerica. "He chose an impetuous land of history," Cuadra writes of Aldana, while he was chronicling his own dutiful infatuation with that "fistful of salt in the vast tropical greenness" that is Granada, Nicaragua.

**Avital Gad-Cykman**'s flash collection will be published by Matter Press in September 2014. Her stories have also appeared in *The Literary Review, Glimmer Train, McSweeney's, Prism International, Other Voices*, and *Michigan Quarterly Review*. She is the winner of the Margaret Atwood Studies magazine prize for non-fiction, a four-time Pushcart prize nominee and a finalist for the Iowa Fiction Award for story collections.

**Catherine Daly** has lived in the four corners of the United States of America as well as in the center. Her most recent book, *Seedbed / Controller*, published by limit cycle press, is available free online, and in print through Amazon. She is author of nine books of poetry, and has one forthcoming, *Cookery*.

**Rubén Dario** was born in Nicaragua in 1867 and died there in 1916, following an ill-advised lecture tour of North America. Octavio Paz once described Modernism, the poetic movement in Spanish of which Dario became the leader, as "a dancing class, a gymnasium, a circus, and a masked ball." Paz went on to say that "everything written in Spanish after Modernism has been affected in one way or another by that great renascence," and that "Dario was not only the richest and most ample of the Modernist poets: he was one of the great modern poets."

**Arturo Desimone** (b. 1984) is a writer and visual artist currently living between the Netherlands and Argentina, after being born and raised on Aruba, a son of refugees. His visual art is an apocalyptic bestiary concerned with themes of love, faith, political rebellion, his manner of drawing intuitive, between an illiterate poetry and visual narratives, myth-informed. The Spanish translation of his book of poems *About a Lover from Tunisia* will be published this year as *La Amada de Túnez* by the Argentinian independent publisher Audisea. His drawings have been exhibited in galleries in the Netherlands such as Kers Gallery. He is at work on a long fiction project. His poetry and short fiction have appeared in the *New Orleans Review, Acentos, African Writing, Hamilton Stone* and *Knot*, and he has poetry translations forthcoming in *Blue Lyra Review*.

**Antonio Gonçalves Dias** (b. 1823) was the illegitimate son of a Portuguese shopkeeper and a Brazilian *cafusa*, a woman of mixed Indian and African heritage. He spent his childhood with his mother on a small cotton farm near Porto das Caixas, and then travelled to Portugal with his father in 1837. While he was studying law and modern languages at the University of Coimbra, he wrote "Song of Exile," which has often been referred to as the most famous poem in the Portuguese language. Dias was drowned in the Baia do Cumã during an 1864 shipwreck of which he was the only casualty.

**Jesse Dorris**' work has appeared in *T, Time, All Things Considered, Slate, and Conjunctions*, among other places. He and Jaime Manrique co-edited the Lambda Literary Award-nominated anthology *Bésame Mucho: New Gay Latino Fiction*. He lives in Brooklyn.

**Norman Dubie**'s most recent collection of poems, *The Quotations of Bone*, will be published by Copper Canyon Press this Christmas.

**Joseph Duemer** has published three books of poetry, most recently *Magical Thinking* from Ohio St. Univ. Press. His poems have also appeared in *American Poetry Review, The Georgia Review*, and *The Iowa Review*. He has held grants from the NEA and the NEH and has been a Fulbright Senior Research Fellow in Hanoi, Vietnam. He is Professor of Literature at Clarkson University in northern New York.

**Simon Peter Eggertsen** has degrees in literature, language (BYU) and law (Virginia and Cambridge). His pedigree in poetry is recent. His verses have been published in *Nimrod*, *Vallum* (Canada), *New Millennium Writings*, *Ekphrasis*, and elsewhere. His first chapbook, *Memories as Contraband*, will be published by Finishing Line Press in September 2014.

**Paul Éluard** was the pseudonym of Eugène Grindel (born December 14, 1895, Saint-Denis, Paris, France; died November 18, 1952, Charenton-le-Pont), who, along with Louis Aragon, André Breton and others, founded the Surrealist movement, which Éluard later rejected. In 1926, he published *Capitale de la Douleur*, followed by *Poésie et Vérité* (1942), *Poésie Ininterrompue* and *Le Dur Désir de Durer*, illustrated by Marc Chagall (1946).

**Hugh Fox** (1932–2011) published 100 books, *Defiance* (Higgamus Hill Press, 2007) among the most recent. Founder of COSMEP, the International Organization of Independent Publishers, former editor of *Ghost Dance: the International Quarterly of Experimental Poetry*, he was also a contributing reviewer to *Small Press Review* and *SMR*.

**Skip Fox** has published a number of multi-genre works classified as poetry as well as a selected poems (Univ. of New Orleans Press). His novel *wired to zone* will be published by Lavender Ink in the new year.

**Suzanne Frischkorn** is the author of *Lit Windowpane* (2008) and *Girl on a Bridge* (2010) both from Main Street Rag Publishing. In addition, she is the author of five chapbooks. Her honors include the Aldrich Poetry Award for her chapbook *Spring Tide*, selected by Mary Oliver, an Emerging Writers Fellowship, from The Writers Center, and an Individual Artist Fellowship from the Connecticut Commission of Culture and Tourism. She serves as an assistant poetry editor for *Anti-*.

**Tess Gallagher**'s 9th poetry collection is *Midnight Lantern: New & Selected Poems* from Graywolf Press. She lives and writes in Pt. Angeles, WA, and in the Northwest of Ireland in Co. Sligo.

**Anne Germanacos**'s collection of short stories, *In the Time of the Girls*, was published by BOA Editions in 2010. Her novel *Tribute* was published by Rescue Press (2014). Together with her husband, she ran the Ithaka Cultural Study Program in Greece on the islands of Kalymnos and Crete. She runs the Germanacos Foundation in San Francisco.

**John Gilgun**, author of *Everything That Has Been Shall Be Again: The Reincarnation Fables of John Gilgun*, *The Moby Dick Poems*, and other books, retired after 39 years as a college teacher in May 1999 and immediately decided to become a full-time artist. You can see his art if you are on Facebook. Or you can request to be his Facebook Friend and when he approves it you will have access to all of his art.

**Larry Goodell** was born in Roswell, educated in L.A. and Albuquerque, and has been living in Placitas since 1963. His wife is the photographer and phenologist Lenore Goodell. He has been called the Aristophanes of the Upper Sonoran Desert, based on his groundbreaking performances that use hand-made ceremonial items, masks, backdrops, costumes, scrolls and other backings for poems. His satire gets him labeled a "Co(s)mic Clown" but in reality he's as serious as all get out. about.me/larrygoodell is a link to much of his work.

**David Graham** has published six collections of poetry, including *Stutter Monk* and *Second Wind*. He also co-edited (with Kate Sontag) the essay anthology *After Confession: Poetry as Confession*. Essays, reviews, and individual poems have appeared widely, both in print and online. He is Professor of English at Ripon College, where he has also run the Visiting Writers Series for twenty-eight years.

Although **Terri Lee Hackman** was raised amidst orange groves and palm trees in broiling Southern California, she lives in a stone house next to an old castle in rainy, windy North Wales. In the house, her geeky husband's computers are everywhere; her smart daughter's books and art are piled and strewn; their sagacious cat keeps empty boxes for respite.

**John Haines** (1924–2011) was poet and essayist, painter and Alaskan homesteader. His collections of poetry include *Winter News* (1966); *The Stone Harp* (1971); *Cicada* (1977); *News from the Glacier: Selected Poems 1960—980* (1982); *New Poems 1980–1988* (1990), which received the Lenore Marshall Poetry Award. The poems included here were first published in *Porch* in 1980, and in 1979 his long essay, *The Writer As Alaskan*, was published in the Inland Boat pamphlet series by Porch Publications.

**H. Palmer Hall** (1942–2013) was the author of several books of poetry, fiction, and non-fiction, among them *Coming to Terms Foreign and Domestic, Deep Thicket & Still Waters*, and *To Wake Again*. His work appeared in *North American Review, The Texas Observer, Palo Alto Review*, and other literary reviews and anthologies. He was a librarian at St. Mary's University in San Antonio, Texas, where he founded Pecan Grove Press.

**Ed Harkness** is the author of two full-length collections of poems, *Saying the Necessary* (2000) and *Beautiful Passing Lives* (2010), both from Pleasure Boat Studio press. He lives in Shoreline, Washington.

**Charles Hartman** has published eight books of poetry, including *New & Selected Poems*, and three critical books. His textbook *Verse: An Introduction to Prosody*, will be published by Wiley-Blackwell late in 2014. He teaches at Connecticut College.

**James Hawley** (now writing & publishing as "Jim Heavily") is the Poetry Editor at *Hinchas de Poesía*, an online journal based in Los Angeles, & has degrees from Arizona State University & Columbia University. In addition to *The Salt River Review*, his poems have appeared in *Waxwing, The Tule Review, poeticdiversity* and *The Iowa Review*, among others; his poems have been translated into Romanian & appeared in *Vatra Veche*. He spends his days in the backyard watching the Cessnas & Piper Cubs take off & land at Sacramento Executive Airport.

**Bob Herz** is author of two books of poetry, editor of *Nine Mile Magazine*, and publisher of the W.D. Hoffstadt series of poetry books. He lives and works in Syracuse, NY.

**Dennis Hinrichsen** is the author of six books of poems. His most recent are *Rip-tooth* (2010 Tampa Poetry Prize) and *Kurosawa's Dog* (2008 FIELD Poetry Prize). He lives in Lansing, MI.

**Cynthia Hogue**'s eighth collection of poetry is entitled *Revenance* (Red Hen Press, 2014). She teaches in the MFA Program at Arizona State University, and lives with her husband, the French economist Sylvain Gallais, in Phoenix.

**Christopher Howell** has published ten collections of poems, most recently *Gaze* (Milkweed Editions, 2012) and *Dreamless and Possible: poems New and Selected* (University of Washington Press, 2010). He teaches at Eastern Washington University.

**Laura Jensen** lives in Tacoma, Washington. She adjunct-taught in the 1980s, organized a poetry series (1994–1996) and delivered newspapers (1999–2004). A non-parent, she walks, bikes, and uses transit. She blogs at library computers and volunteers at Pacific Lutheran University's Scandinavian Archives. Her books include *Bad Boats* (Ecco Press 1978), and *Memory* (1982) and *Shelter* (1985) from Dragon Gate.

**Halvard Johnson** has received grants and fellowships from the National Endowment for the Arts, the Maryland State Arts Council, the Woodrow Wilson Foundation, and other sources. He has lived and taught in Chicago; El Paso; Cayey, Puerto Rico; Washington, D.C.; Baltimore; and New York City. Currently, he lives with his wife, prize-winning writer and visual artist Lynda Schor, in San Miguel de Allende, Guanajuato, Mexico.

The author of nine books, **Tsipi Keller** is the recipient of several literary awards, including National Endowment for the Arts Fellowships, and New York Foundation for the Arts grants. Her most recent publication is the novel *Elsa* (2014).

**Jesse Lee Kercheval** is the author of 13 books of poetry, fiction and memoir including the novel *My Life as a Silent Movie* and the poetry collection *Cinema Muto*. She is also a translator, specializing in Uruguayan poetry.

**Edith Konecky** has published six books, all still in print, the most widely read of which is *Allegra Maud Goldman*. Four others are novels and the fifth a collection of her previously published short stories. She is a native New Yorker.

**Nathan Leslie**'s seven books of short fiction include *Madre, Believers, Drivers, and Sibs* (just published by Aqueous Books in the spring of 2014). He is also the author of *Night Sweat*, a poetry collection. His first novel, *The Tall Tale of Tommy Twice*, was published by Atticus Books in 2012.

**Norman Lock**'s recent books include *Pieces for Small Orchestra & Other Fictions* (Spuyten Duyvil Press), *Grim Tales* (Mud Luscious Press/Dzanc Books), *Love Among the Particles* and the new novel *The Boy in His Winter* (both from Bellevue Literary Press). More at normanlock.com.

In 1921 **Federico García Lorca** was in the shallows of what was to be an extraordinarily sustained implosion of poetic activity that would last for more than a decade. He had just simultaneously begun two books, one of which, *Suites*, not published until 1983, would eventually contain a number of lyrics so completely hermetic they might have collapsed in on themselves like windless sails if not for the fact that the poet's persona was wide enough to absorb and reflect in silver moonlight the geographical and mythical landscape of Andalucía in its entirety. "Widow of the Moon" is from *Suites*. García Lorca was murdered by the side of a road in 1936 during the Spanish Civil War.

**John Morgan** has published five books of poetry, most recently *River of Light: A Conversation with Kabir*, as well as a collection of essays. In addition to *Porch* and *Salt River Review*, his poems have appeared in *The New Yorker, Poetry, APR, The New Republic, The Paris Review*, and many other magazines.

By day **Peter Munro** counts fish, conducting research fishing cruises in the Bering Sea, the Gulf of Alaska, and the Aleutian Islands. After the field season they chain him to a computer in Seattle, permitting occasional visits to his wife and children between parameter estimations. By night, Munro makes poems, some of which have been published in the likes of *Poetry, Beloit Poetry Journal, Iowa Review, Birmingham Poetry Review, Crab Creek Review*, and *Poetry East*. Munro offers a full refund at munropoetry.com.

**Sheila Murphy**'s most recent book-length publications feature collaborative visual poetry: *Yes It Is* (with John M. Bennett; Luna Bisonte Prods. 2014); *2 Juries + 2 Storeys = 4 Stories Toujours* (with K.S. Ernst; Xerolage 55 from Xexoxial Editions, 2013).

**Pablo Neruda** [b. 1904] served as an honorary Chilean consul to Burma from 1927 to 1933, during which time he advanced the cause of world trade not very much, but managed to compose a seminal work of modern poetry, *Residencia en la tierra* [Residence on Earth]. During a long and active life, Neruda kissed many women, married some, and wrote many excellent books, not the least of which is his final one, *Fin de mundo* [World's End]. Neruda was also fortunate enough to become, however briefly, a valued friend and peer of Federico García Lorca's. Neruda died of leukemia in 1973.

**Carol Novack** (1948–2011) founded the *Mad Hatters' Review* in 2005 and later founded the non-profit arts organization, MadHat, Inc. She was also the curator of reading series at KGB Bar in New York. *Giraffes in Hiding: The Mythical Memoirs of Carol Novack*, which Hugh Fox called "THE most seductive, original, impacting work I have seen for years," was published in Fall 2010 by Spuyten Duyvil Press.

**Sergio Ortiz** is an educator, poet, photographer, painter, and founding editor of *Undertow Tanka Review*. He lives in San Juan Puerto Rico. He is a four-time nominee for the 2010–2011 Sundress Best of the Web Anthology, and a two-time 2010 Pushcart nominee.

**Sam Pereira** was born in Los Banos, CA, on an Easter Sunday in 1949. He received his BA from California State University, Fresno, and his MFA from the University of Iowa Writers' Workshop. His books include *The Marriage of the Portuguese—Expanded Edition*, from Tagus Press at the University of Massachusetts, Dartmouth; *Brittle Water*, a limited edition from Abattoir Editions/Penumbra Press at the University of Nebraska, Omaha, and two from Tebot Bach, *A Café in Boca* and *Dusting on Sunday*. He is currently completing a new manuscript and is an English teacher in California's great San Joaquin Valley.

**Ignacio Ruiz Perez** is a promising young poet from Tuxla, Gutiérrez, Mexico. He has published articles in *La Palabra y el Hombre* and *Columbre*. He was awarded the National Poetry Prize Alí Chumacero in 2000. He is the author of *Ejecuciones* (2002) and *La canción de los desterrados* [Song of the Exiles](2004). More recently he was awarded the Premio Rodulfo Figueroa 2005 for his book of poems *La señal del cuervo*.

**Fernando Pessoa** (1888–1935 in Lisboa): "… intelligence, an errant fiction of the surface. Material life is either pure dream or a mere ensemble of atoms, oblivious to our rational conclusions and our emotional motivations. And so the essence of life is an illusion, an appearance, which is either pure being or non-being, and the illusion or appearance that it's nothing must belong to non-being—life is death. How vain is all our striving to create, under the spell of the illusion of not dying! But the material cooling down of earth will carry off not only the living who cover it, but also … A Homer or a Milton can do no more than a comet that strikes the earth." [From *The Book of Disquiet*, translated by Richard Zenith.]

The *Salt River Review* & *Porch* Anthology

**Tim Poland** lives and works in the New River Valley near the Blue Ridge Mountains in southwestern Virginia. He is the author of a novel, *The Safety of Deeper Water* (Vandalia Press/West Virginia University Press, 2009), *Escapee* (America House, 2001), a collection of short fiction, and *Other Stones, Kinder Temples* (Pudding House, 2008), a chapbook of poems. His work has appeared widely in various literary magazines.

**Tiffany Promise** was involved in the writing programs at both Sarah Lawrence College and Eugene Lang College, where she received her BA in writing and literature. She received her MFA from CalArts, where she completed a novel-length manuscript filled with creepily beautiful poetic fiction. She likes Disneyland, comic books, cats, and the macabre.

**Doug Ramspeck** is the author of four poetry books. His most recent collection, *Original Bodies*, was selected for the Michael Waters Poetry Prize and is published by Southern Indiana Review Press. Individual poems have appeared in journals that include *The Kenyon Review, The Southern Review*, and *The Georgia Review*.

**Rochelle Ratner** (1949–2008) published two novels and fourteen books of poetry, including *House and Home, The Lion's Share, Balancing Acts*, and *Combing The Waves*. She lived in New York City, where she was Executive Editor of *American Book Review* and reviewed regularly for *Library Journal*. An anthology she edited, *Bearing Life: Women's Writings on Childlessness*, was published in January 2000 by The Feminist Press.

**Carlos Reyes**'s latest works are *Pomegranate, Sister of the Heart; Poems* (2013), *Poemas de amor y locura / Poems of Love and Madness; Selected Translations* (2014). Last year he was a fellow at the Fundación Valparaíso (Mojácar, Spain), and Poet-in-resident at Acadia National Park (Maine) and Devils Tower National Monument (Wyoming).

**Tad Richards**' most recent novel, *Nick & Jake*, came out in 2013. He is president and artistic director of Opus 40 Sculpture Park and Museum in Saugerties, NY. Recent anthology publications include *Villanelles*, edited by Annie Finch and Marie-Elzabeth Mali, and *The Book of Forms*, Fourth Edition, by Lewis Turco.

**Peter Robertson** is an author and literary translator based in Buenos Aires and London. He is founder and president of the literary journal *Interlitq* at interlitq.org.

**Carole Rosenthal**'s fiction and nonfiction appears in many places, and she is the author of the short story collection *It Doesn't Have To Be Me* (Hamilton Stone Editions). Her stories have been in a wide variety of magazines, including *Able Muse, ACM, the minnesota riview, Confrontation, Other Voices, The Cream City Review*, and *Mother Jones*. Rosenthal's writing, often anthologized, has been dramatized for radio and television and translated into eleven languages. She is a longtime professor at Pratt Institute, and lives part-time in New York City and part-time in the Catskills Mountains.

**Mary Ruefle**'s latest book is *Trances Of The Blast* (Wave Books, 2013). She lives in Vermont.

**Thaddeus Rutkowski**'s latest novel, *Haywire*, was a fiction finalist in the 2013 Asian American Literary Awards, and it won the Members' Choice Award. He received a fiction fellowship from the New York Foundation for the Arts.

**Lynda Schor** has had 6 collections of short fiction published, and her stories have appeared in a variety of magazines and literary journals. Her most recent collection is *Sexual Harassment Rules* (Spuyten Duyvil). She has won several grants, including two Maryland State Arts Council Grants, a Baltimore City Arts Grant, and received fellowships from the Ragdale Foundation, The MacDowell Foundation, Virginia Center for the Creative Arts, and others. She taught in the Writing Program of The New School for 25 years. Currently she lives with her husband, Halvard Johnson, a poet, and their two dogs, Natasha and Koki, in San Miguel de Allende, Guanajuato, Mexico.

**Icy Sedgwick** was born in the North East of England, and lives and works in Newcastle. Icy had her first book, a pulp Western named *The Guns of Retribution*, published in 2011, and her horror fantasy, *The Necromancer's Apprentice*, was released in March 2014. She spends her non-writing time working on a PhD in Film Studies, considering the use of set design in contemporary horror.

Since her first fiction publication—which was in *The Salt River Review*—**Gail Louise Siegel**'s work has appeared across the web and in print, from *Ascent*, *Elm Leaves* and *FRiGG*, to Matter Press, *Post Road* and *Wigleaf*. She has an MFA from Bennington College and lives in Evanston, Illinois.

In 1983 Raymond Carver chose **Jim Simmerman**'s (1952–2006) poetry for a Pushcart Prize and proclaimed: "… Simmerman is clearly among the best poets of his generation." As accolades piled up, Simmerman published five books in his and co-edited *Dog Music*. He remained anchored to Flagstaff, volunteering at the local high schools and reading at businesses and bookstores right down the street from his home. *Last & Selected Poems of Jim Simmerman* will be published by Gorsky Press in 2015.

For a number of years in the late 1970s, **Greg Simon** was the Northwest and Review Editor of *Porch*, and later an associate editor for Trask House Books and *The Salt River Review*. He is the co-translator, with Steven F. White, of Federico García Lorca's *Poet in New York* [1988]; Gaston Baquero's *Angel of Rain* [2006]; Pablo Antonio Cuadra's *Seven Trees Against the Dying Light* [2007]; and Rubén Dario's *Selected Poems* [2005]. His most recent writing projects include a book of lyrics adapted from the writings of Fernando Pessoa and his three favorite heteronyms: Alberto Caeiro, Álvaro de Campos, and Ricardo Reis; and a selection of the early poems of Anna Akhmatova. He lives and works in Portland, Oregon.

**Emeniano Acain Somoza, Jr.** considers himself the official spiritual advisor of his roommates, Gordot and Dwight—the first a goldfish, the other a Turkish Van cat. His works have been Editor's Choice in *The Poetry Magazine* and featured in the *Moria Poetry Journal*, *Fogged Clarity*, *The Buddhist Poetry Review*, and elsewhere. His first book, *A Fistful of Moonbeams*, was published by Kilmog Press in April 2010. He is busy anthologizing emptiness and boredom at the moment while working as an Academic Admissions Specialist somewhere in the land of camels and cactuses.

**Adam J. Sorkin** is a translator of contemporary Romanian poetry. His recent books include Dan Sociu's *Mouths Dry with Hatred* (Longleaf Press) and Rodica Draghincescu's *A Sharp Double-Edged Luxury Object* (Červená Barva Press).

**David Starkey** served as Santa Barbara's 2009–2010 Poet Laureate and is Director of the Creative Writing Program at Santa Barbara City College. His poetry has appeared in many journals, including *The American Scholar*, *The Georgia Review* and *The Southern Review*, and in seven full-length collections, most recently *It Must Be Like the World*, *Circus Maximus*, and *Like a Soprano*.

**Pamela Stewart** recently published a chapbook, *Just Visiting*, with Grey Suit Editions, London. She lives on a farm in western Massachusetts.

**Carolyn Stoloff**'s most recent collection, *Reaching for Honey*, was published by Red Hen Press. Her forthcoming collection, *Ah Wind*, published by MadHat Press, will be out this year.

"You don't escape into poetry," **Mark Strand** told a recent interviewer. "You confront yourself." The peripatetic poet, who was born on Prince Edward Island in 1934 and who has collected every major American literary award available to poets, recently retired from teaching, and now lives on a quiet street in Madrid. He will publish his *Collected Poems* with Knopf in the fall of 2014. "If I have a country," Strand told another interviewer, "it is the English language."

**Lynn Strongin** (b. 1939) is of the dirty thirties, grew up in New York in the forties. Four or five years ago her work was nominated for the Pulitzer Prize in Literature. The late, great Hugh Fox has called her the most exciting poet writing in he language today.

**Jeanie Thompson**'s books of poems include *How to Enter the River, Litany for a Vanishing Landscape, Witness, White for Harvest: New and Selected Poems*, and most recently *The Seasons Bear Us*. She is founding director of the Alabama Writers' Forum, a statewide service organization for literary arts, and a member of the poetry faculty in the Spalding University brief-residency MFA Writing Program. Poems from her book-length persona poem project, "The Myth of Water; Poems From the Life of Helen Keller," appeared recently in *KROnline, The New Sound, The Louisville Review*, and *PoemMemoirStory*.

**Girija Tropp**, an Australian writer, has had so many short fictions published in the United States that she believes in previous lives over there. Most recently, her microfiction has appeared in *New World Writing, SmokeLong Quarterly*, and anthologised in *Café Irreal*.

**Marina Tsvetayeva**'s life (1892–1941), perhaps the most tragic of the Russian poets, involved extremes of wealth and poverty, with ostracism from both sides of the political divide. Her father, a foremost Russian art historian, had founded the Pushkin Museum of Fine Art in Moscow, and the family lost everything in the aftermath of the Revolution. During her lengthy Paris émigré period, she became a pariah due to her husband's (a former White Army officer) collaboration with the Soviet secret police, including suspected participation in assassinations. Their flight back to the Soviet Union, ahead of the Nazi occupation of France, resulted in her husband's execution, son's arrest and long imprisonment, and her own starvation and eventual suicide.

**Liliana Ursu** is a prominent Romanian poet. Her most recent book in English, *A Path to the Sea*, translated by Ursu, Sorkin and Gallagher (Pleasure Boat Studio), was awarded the Silver Prize in poetry for 2011, ForeWord Reviews.

**Donna Vitucci** works too many hours at two different jobs that keep her hopping. Moreover, they keep her from her stories and her characters, and some kind of reckoning must be looming. Her past work (when she had more time) can be found at dozens of places online and in print.

**Zachary Watterson**'s essay "Open Late Hours" was listed as a notable essay in *Best American Essays* 2013. His short stories and essays have appeared in *Massachusetts Review*, *River Styx*, *The Stranger*, *Commentary Magazine*, and *Post Road*. His work has been anthologized in India and published in the UK and he has received fellowships and awards from the Bread Loaf Writers' Conference and the Elizabeth George Foundation.

**Roger Weingarten**, author of ten collections of poetry & co-editor of seven poetry anthologies, has lectured, taught & read at writers' conferences, poetry festivals, & universities nationally & internationally. Founder & Senior Professor in the MFA in Writing & the Postgraduate Writers' Conference at Vermont College from 1980–2008, his awards include a Pushcart Prize, a *Louisville Review* Poetry Prize, a National Endowment for the Arts Award, & an Ingram Merrill Foundation Award in Literature. His poems, stories, & essays have appeared in *The New Yorker*, *APR*, *Poetry East*, *The Paris Review*, and *Poetry*, among many other journals & anthologies. His eleventh collection, *The Four Gentlemen and their Footman*, will be published by Longleaf in 2015.

**Steven F. White** is the author of *Bajo la palabra de las plantas: poesía selecta* (1979–2009), the editor of *El consumo de lo que somos: muestra de poesía ecológica hispánica contemporánea* and *Ayahuasca Reader: Encounters with the Amazon's Sacred Vine*, as well as the translator (with Greg Simon) of Federico García Lorca's *Poet in New York*.

**Kulpreet Yadav**'s latest crime novel, *Catching the Departed*, was shortlisted by Hachette-DNA in the contest Hunt for the Next Bestseller & launched at The Arts House, Singapore on 18 July 2014. He is the Founder-Editor of *Open Road Review* & lives in Delhi.

POSTSCRIPT:

Shortly before this volume went into production, we learned of the death of Mark Strand (April 11, 1934–November 29, 2014), who was teacher, mentor, and friend to some of us as early as 1967 at the University of Washington. We thank him and remember him here.

Printed by Libri Plureos GmbH in Hamburg, Germany